UNDERSTANDING CHILDREN

PREPARED FOR THE COURSE TEAM
BY LUCY RAI AND RONNY FLYNN

The Open University, Walton Hall, Milton Keynes MK7 6AA

First published 2004, reprinted 2006

Edited, designed and typeset by The Open University

Printed in the United Kingdom by CPI, Oxford

ISBN 0 7492 6840 9
1.2

This publication forms part of an Open University course, Y156 *Understanding Children*. Details of this and other Open University courses can be obtained from the Course Information and Advice Centre, PO Box 724, The Open University, Milton Keynes MK7 6ZS, United Kingdom; tel. +44 (0)1908 653231; email general-enquiries@open.ac.uk

Alternatively, you may visit the Open University website at www.open.ac.uk where you can learn more about the wide range of courses and packs offered at all levels by The Open University.

To purchase a selection of Open University course materials visit the webshop at www.ouw.co.uk, or contact Open University Worldwide, Michael Young Building, Walton Hall, Milton Keynes MK7 6AA, United Kingdom, for a brochure; tel. +44 (0)1908 858785; fax +44 (0)1908 858787; email ouwenq@open.ac.uk

COURSE TEAM

TEAM

Lucy Rai, Chair, Author
Ronny Flynn, Author
George Marsh, Course Manager
Peter Barnes
Pat Spoors
Penny Wilkinson, Course Secretary

CRITICAL READERS

Rachel Burr, Open University
Jabeer Butt, formerly Race Equality Unit
Janet Collins, Open University
Trevor Evans, Openings Tutor
Sue Griffin, National Childminding Association
Sarah Lambert, Blackpool Local Education Authority
Penny Lancaster, Coram Family
Sheila Lockwood, City of Birmingham Local Education Authority
Liz Malcolm, London Borough of Lewisham
Jacqueline Mann, South West Peninsula Strategic Health Authority
Linda Miller, Open University
Andy Northedge, Open University
Carol Ulanowsky, Open University

DEVELOPMENTAL TESTERS

Ali Ni Charraighe
Charlotte Dodson
Jacqui Dodson
Pat Duncomb
Hazel Kennedy
Grace Quinn
Charlotte Walton, Openings Tutor

EXTERNAL ASSESSOR

Dr Rennie Johnston, Southampton University

PRODUCTION TEAM

Deb Bywater, Courses Office Manager, Production and Logistics
Debbie Crouch, Graphic Designer
Barbara Fraser, Picture Researcher
Sue Glover, Editor
Mike Levers, Photographer
Deana Plummer, Picture Researcher
Sarah Shepherd, Media Account Manager

A WORD FROM THE AUTHORS

The authors of *Understanding Children* are Lucy Rai and Ronny Flynn.

RONNY FLYNN

I am a lecturer in 'Children, young people and families' and mother of a 12-year-old daughter, Kiran. I have a background that includes Indian, Scottish and Irish. My daughter thinks I should practise what I write about a little more – and not get so 'stressy' about work.

LUCY RAI

I am a lecturer in the Centre for Widening Participation but in my past life have worked as a social worker. My husband and I have two little boys, who are dual heritage (Nepalese and Scots/Irish). They are aged 4 and 6 and have taught me (nearly) everything I know!

ACKNOWLEDGEMENTS

The course team would like to acknowledge all of the contributors to this course:

All those at Cottesbrooke Infants School in Birmingham, particularly Ann Phillips (headteacher), Alison Everette, Elliott, Paige, Zobia, Megan, Aliya, and Corey

All those at Birmingham Education Department, particularly Andrew Cooper

All those who took part in the case study family 'photo shoot': Julie Gowan, Jim Bailey, Kiran Flynn, Kal Rai, Olivia and Sam Marshall, Aaron and Angie Clapp, Fay Scriven, Pat Chalk, Beth Soman, Vicky Akehurst and Imtiaaz Butt

All those who contributed examples and personal accounts: Louise Hutt, Oliver Hutt, Marea Saunders, Hazel Kennedy, Julie Clifford, Jo Dawson

The BBC production team for *A Child of Our Time* (BBC TV, 2001)

Advice and guidance on the integration of study skills: Dr Theresa Lillis, Maureen Haywood, Maggie Coates

CONTENTS

INTRODUCTION   **7**

THE AIMS OF THIS COURSE   7

MEET THE FAMILY   9

UNIT 1   BABIES BEING HEARD   **15**

1   PEOPLE RIGHT FROM THE START   15

1.1 Babies are people too!   16

1.2 Watching babies   24

1.3 Promoting development   27

1.4 Difference and young children   31

1.5 Different babies, different families   35

1.6 Conclusion   39

2   SECURE RELATIONSHIPS   40

2.1 The value of close relationships   41

2.2 Promoting close relationships   47

2.3 Important others   49

2.4 Managing relationships   51

2.5 Conclusion   53

APPENDIX TO UNIT 1   55

UNIT 2   CHILDREN HAVING A SAY   **63**

1   NEGOTIATIONS AT HOME   63

1.1 Bedtimes   64

1.2 Helping children talk about feelings   74

1.3 Power and parenting   79

1.4 Conclusion   84

2   NEGOTIATIONS AT SCHOOL   86

2.1 Moving from home to school   86
2.2 Challenging expectations   88
2.3 Expectations in school   92
2.4 Health in school: policy and reality   104
2.5 Conclusion   111

UNIT 3 YOUNG PEOPLE FINDING THEIR PLACE   116

1   CHILDREN AND DECISIONS   116

1.1 Having a say and being heard   117
1.2 Putting it into practice   119

2   WHAT CHILDREN WANT FROM FAMILY LIFE AND WORK   123

2.1 Views on family life   123
2.2 Working parents and family life   127
2.3 Communication and consultation about family life 133

3   CHILDREN'S CONTRIBUTIONS TO FAMILY LIFE   134

3.1 Children do more than adults think   135
3.2 Caring tasks and emotional support   140
3.3 Looking further afield   141
3.4 What skills are children learning?   144

4   CHILDREN AND FRIENDSHIPS   146

4.1 Having friends   147
4.2 Being friends   147
4.3 What friends do together   148
4.4 The importance of 'just hanging out'   150
4.5 Patterns of friendship   152

CONCLUSION   156

REFERENCES   157

ACKNOWLEDGEMENTS   160

INTRODUCTION

THE AIMS OF THIS COURSE

The course aims to develop your:

- understanding of ways to promote confidence, growth and self-esteem in children aged 0–11 years
- understanding of how to develop consistent, open and honest communication with children across the age range
- ability to study effectively in order to undertake further higher education courses.

Welcome to *Understanding Children*! We hope that you will enjoy the learning offered in the pages ahead. As we write we are assuming that you have an interest in children and in developing your confidence to study at a higher education level. Beyond that we imagine that readers are all very different – in age, background (for example, ethnicity and social class), language, experience and employment. Maybe you have worked for many years with children, maybe you have children of your own – but perhaps neither of these applies and you have an interest in understanding children more. Your own experience – and we all have some experience, for example of having been children ourselves and living in society alongside children – will be as valuable to you as the study materials here. You will be asked to stop and think or reflect on your experiences many times through the course.

The objective of teaching an 'understanding' of 'children' is an ambitious one in a short course. As you move through the course you will focus on children in three age groups.

- Unit 1 deals with babies, what they are capable of and their important relationships.
- Unit 2 deals with 4- to 5-year-old children's experiences of having a say both in the family and when starting school.
- Unit 3 looks at the contributions of 10- to 11-year-olds to family life, and their friendships with other children.

Understanding Children is not intended to be a comprehensive account of how children grow and develop. However, a reflection on the capabilities and experiences of children between 0 and 11 would be very limited without some recognition of how children grow and learn to interact with the society around them. All of the units develop a common theme of *communication* – the ways in which children at different ages communicate their feelings and wishes, and the ways in which adults respond to them.

In *Understanding Children* we have tried to use children's voices and experiences wherever we can. It has also been important to reflect the diversity of families in the UK in the course materials. Minority ethnic groups make up about nine per cent of the population in England. A significant percentage of families have a disabled adult or child member. Some reduction in prejudice in society has meant that families where adults are lesbian or gay are able to be more open about who they are. One third of households in England and Wales include dependant children and nearly one in four of these are lone-parent families (92.2% of these headed by mothers). More than one in ten children live in a stepfamily and eleven per cent live with unmarried cohabiting couples. This is the reality of children's lives in British society, and we hope that this rich diversity has been reflected throughout the course.

Before we make a start on these topics, we would like to ask you to think about what you want to get out of this course in terms of developing your confidence in studying. You will notice that one of the aims of *Understanding Children* is to enable you to develop your ability to study effectively in order to undertake further higher education courses.

As you work through the course you will come across discussion intended to help you develop your ability to study effectively and with greater confidence. These *effective study* discussion points allow you to think about how you learn, and the most effective and useful ways of studying. They form an important part of your learning and we hope that you find the discussion enjoyable and interesting. We believe that taking time to think about how you study and learn will assist you in getting the most out of the course, while learning more about different aspects of children. Many people, even those who have already dipped a toe into higher education, may not have had the opportunity to reflect upon this aspect of study, so here is your chance!

There are six *effective study* areas:

- Reading for study

- Collecting and using evidence

- Reflection

- Evaluating ideas

- Essay writing

- Developing and demonstrating understanding

You will come across each of these areas once in each unit, usually attached to a learning activity, but not necessarily in the order that they appear here. The *effective study* areas are interconnected and you will move from developing in one area to another. Your reading/listening/viewing will provide the ideas for you to 'understand' and reflect upon. Your own thoughts should enable you to collect and evaluate evidence and then compare ideas from different sources. You will demonstrate all of these stages when you come to write your essay. We encourage you to include the *effective study* sections as you will be required to think and write about how your ability to study is developing in each of the three assignments. Get into the habit of filing your notes on these activities in a separate file divided into six sections, one for each area of *effective study*. You will also find that there is an *effective study* review activity at the end of each unit, which should be handed in to your tutor as the study section of your assignments. Keeping your *effective study* notes in one place should make it easier to complete these activities.

What's all this stuff?

If this book is the first thing that you have opened, then wait a moment before you read on! You have lots of items included in your mailing and you should begin by checking you have everything using the contents checklist provided. Then read your Course Guide, which will help you work out what it is all for and when to use it.

What should I be doing?

Having sorted out all of your materials and made contact with your tutor, you are ready to start reading. Have a blank pad of paper with you while you read, but don't try to copy out the text from this book – no one is going to take the book away from you so you can always come back to it! Divide your notepad page in half and on one side jot down notes on anything you read which strikes you as interesting or important. On the other side, just as importantly, write down any thoughts, ideas or memories which come to mind as you read. You could head this column 'My thoughts'. Your own thinking as you read will not be there for you to come back to and is just as important as the course materials when you come to write an essay.

Now let's introduce you to the case study family ('the Family') who will accompany you through the course.

MEET THE FAMILY

The Family you are about to meet is fictional, but its members will hopefully become believable figures. The Family is used throughout *Understanding Children* as a teaching tool to introduce you to the learning material. The Family is made up from the combined experiences of our families and friends and those we know about from our own and other people's research. You will be exploring and reflecting upon the challenges of understanding children along with the Family – and the children, Daisy, Ryan and Mia, will be there to tell you how they see it. The children represent the three broad age ranges focused on in each unit, so in Unit 1 Mia will take the lead, in Unit 2 it will be Ryan, and in the final unit Daisy will be centre stage.

The case study is here to help you and will make your learning memorable, but you should not feel that the details of the case study are what you are expected to learn; don't try to memorize it!

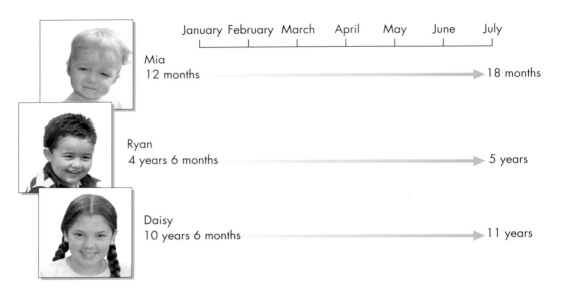

Figure 1 Time line

All of the three units take place in the same six-month period, so over the whole course all of the children will grow up by six months. The ages shown on the left of Figure 1 are the children's ages at the beginning of each unit.

So, here's the Family:

Jodie Watkins	31 years	Part-time recruitment consultant
Eamon McLaughlin	36 years	Full-time telephone engineer (shift work)
Mia Watkins	12 months	Daughter of Jodie and Eamon
Ryan Adunola	4 years 6 months	Son of Jodie Watkins and Graham Adunola
Daisy Adunola	10 years 6 months	Daughter of Jodie Watkins and Graham Adunola
Graham Adunola	30 years	Retail manager
Michael Watkins	62 years	Jodie's father, retired
Grace Watkins	60 years	Jodie's mother, retired
Rosalind Adunola	67 years	Graham's aunt

Families can also be described through drawing a family tree or 'genogram'. Social workers, for example, often use such a pictorial description of a family to help them understand the relationships in a complicated family. Figure 2 shows how the case study Family would look drawn as a genogram. The key will help you to understand the symbols used.

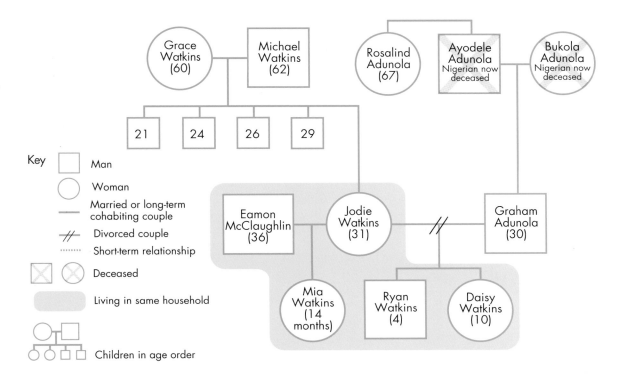

Key

☐ Man

◯ Woman

— Married or long-term cohabiting couple

⫫ Divorced couple

⋯⋯ Short-term relationship

⊠ ⊗ Deceased

▢ Living in same household

Children in age order

Figure 2 Case study Family's genogram (family tree)

YOUR FAMILY TREE

Allow about 15 minutes

Have a go at drawing a genogram for your family. Use the key in Figure 2 to help you. When you have completed it, compare it with the case study Family's genogram. What do you notice?

COMMENT

How did you get on? Did you find that your family was relatively easy to illustrate in this way, or were you surprised at how complex your family appears? Perhaps you were unsure who to include? It is not always easy to decide who to include – for example, Rosalind Adunola is not related to Jodie or Eamon but is a big part of their family life so we have chosen to include her here.

We hope this activity has begun to make you think about the different sort of families that children experience.

Now you know who is in the Family, you will learn a little more about them as people.

MEET THE FAMILY

Daisy and Ryan live with their mum, Jodie, and her partner, Eamon. Jodie divorced Ryan's and Daisy's father when Ryan was 18 months old. It was a reasonably amicable separation. Graham lives about 30 miles away and maintains contact by telephone and regular weekend visits with Daisy and Ryan. He also regularly visits Rosalind, often taking all three children!

Jodie and Eamon have decided not to marry. Eamon has a close relationship with the children and plays a significant role in their care as he works shifts. Mia is Jodie's and Eamon's daughter and her birth has further cemented their relationship. Jodie and Eamon have been determined to involve Daisy and Ryan in the care of their new sister as much as possible. Eamon, however, has felt that he lacks confidence in caring for Mia – he has had little contact with babies and is also anxious about his role with Daisy and Ryan now Mia has arrived. Unlike Jodie, who is one of five children, Eamon is an only child.

Jodie returned to work part-time when Mia was five months old. Mia's care is shared between Jodie's parents (Michael and Grace), Eamon and Jodie. Michael and Grace are very involved in their grandchildren's lives and are interested in thinking and learning about children along with Jodie and Eamon.

The Watkins/McLaughlin household is busy, at times hectic, but generally lively and happy. Jodie and Graham talk on the telephone a lot about their children and how they parent them. All three 'parents' come from very different family backgrounds and believe in talking about and sharing their experiences and cultures to enrich their children's lives.

Jodie's parents are English and originally from London. Jodie is a confident parent; she played a significant role in the care of her four younger brothers and also has six nephews and nieces.

Eamon is from County Antrim in Northern Ireland and Jodie met him after he moved to the Birkenhead area for work. They have been together a couple of years.

Graham has lived in and around Birkenhead all of his life. However, as his parents were Nigerian, he is keen that Daisy and Ryan are positive about their Nigerian background. He sees Rosalind as very important to this as his parents are dead and he has no other Nigerian relatives in the country.

Daisy:

> I'm 10 and will be moving schools next year. I've pretty much grown out of most kids' stuff and my little brother drives me mental – always messing with my stuff. Mia is sweet though – but she is always either asleep or making a racket. Mum and Eamon keep on at me to keep my music down and not to leave stuff around in case she gets hold of it. My best mates are Sammy and Sandeep. We always go around together, shopping, listening to CDs and just hanging out. I'm good at maths, writing stories and football. I hate spelling, netball and Mrs Jones at school!

Figure 3 Daisy

Ryan:

I go to school like Daisy and my friends are Connor, Paul, Nicholas, Emily and Miss Dee. I like Thomas the Tank Engine and Percy and Gordon and the Fat Controller and Power Rangers! My favourite colour is red and I have a bedroom by myself with a picture of Thomas. Mia sleeps with Mum and Eamon and sometimes I go in their bed in the morning but Mia is too noisy so I watch telly. Nan and Grandpa are coming to see me tomorrow when they bring Mia home and Grandpa is going to help me make a dinosaur picture. I can put my top and trousers on but Mum or Daisy do my shoes. My peg at school has a cat on it. Nicholas has a tiger. I like the tiger. Miss Dee says I am good at my numbers. I missed my playtime today when I was playing Power Rangers with Nicholas. Miss Dee says 'no pushing!'

Figure 4 Ryan

Daisy says:

Mia is our little sister – she is only a baby so she can't talk about herself. We know what she likes though! She loves banana and mushy apple and being on the floor playing. She hates potato, drinking from a bottle and sitting in her chair, except at breakfast time. Mia loves people and meets a lot when she goes out with Rosalind and she gets excited when anyone comes to visit and she always pulls my hair. I love having a baby sister.

Figure 5 Mia

Jodie:

My name is Jodie and I am a working mum with three kids. I work part-time as a recruitment consultant and most of the rest of my time is taken up with the family. I am lucky to have lots of help around, including my ex, Graham, who only lives 30 miles away and has his two to stay now and then. My partner Eamon is a great help with the kids, not just Mia. We also have my parents and Rosalind, Graham's auntie, to help out. I'd like to develop my career as most people in recruitment are graduates, so if I want to move on I really need a degree. Now is not the time with the family getting used to a new addition.

Figure 6 Jodie

Eamon:

Hi, I'm Eamon, the live-in lover! Seriously, I am Mia's dad and I hope that Daisy and little Ryan think of me as 'a dad' even though Graham is their real father. I love Jodie to bits – she is the best thing that has happened to me, although it has been a bit of a shock getting used to living with a busy family. I work shifts as a telephone engineer – it works quite well, and Jodie and I can work around each other so that we do not have to rely too much on her parents.

Figure 7 Eamon

Figure 8 Graham

Graham:

I am Daisy's and Ryan's daddy – they still mean the world to me and I really regret that I was not around more for them when Jo-Jo – sorry Jodie – and I were together. We just drifted apart – no one's fault really. It sounds bad to say it, but in many ways things are better now. I love spending time with Ryan and Daisy-May; we can just chill out and do our own thing when they come and visit. Rosalind plays a big part in their lives – she is their link with my history and better at it than I am. I was brought up by my Auntie Ros and she did the job of mum and dad for me. She spends a lot of time with the kids. I am working more steady now – as a retail manager. Jo-Jo is always on the phone about the kids. It is good to talk to her – but she does worry too much. They are good kids.

Figure 9 Grace

Grace:

I am Jodie's mother, and Daisy's, Ryan's and little Mia's Grandma. I suppose I am also her childminder, although that makes it sound very grand. I was brought up in North London – and met my husband Michael there. We moved to Birkenhead soon after the wedding.

Figure 10 Michael

Michael:

I am the human buggy! I use a wheelchair nowadays and sometimes think that wheeling Mia about is all that they need me for [laughing]. Seriously, it is a wonderful opportunity being involved in the grandchildren – I really missed out with Jo-Jo and her brothers. Still – making up for it now. They are a noisy lot sometimes and I wish Eamon would make an honest woman of Jo-Jo – he tells me he will one day!

Figure 11 Rosalind

Rosalind:

I am Auntie Rosalind. I took care of Graham when he was a boy and try to help out where I can with his children. My family is back in Nigeria – but I left so long ago that I am at home here now. I am still in touch with the family back there. It took a bit of time for Jodie and her folks to get used to me, but now she says she can't do without me. It has been easy to include Mia in some of the things I do, and I'm glad to do it. I consider myself a friend of the family, not just Daisy and Ryan. I don't know! Graham calls me the wise old crow – but he was always the cheeky one!

1 BABIES BEING HEARD

1 PEOPLE RIGHT FROM THE START

CORE QUESTIONS

*   What can very young babies do?
*   How can adults and older children involve babies fully in everyday life and help them feel valued?

Figure 12 Mia, with Ryan's and Daisy's drawings of her

In the course introduction, you met the Family and learned a little about them. In this unit you will meet them again and find out some of the things very young babies can do. You will also discover how babies can contribute to family life and relationships from birth. You will look at what they need from other adults and children, and what they can learn. Using video extracts, you will observe and listen to young babies in action and learn from them. If you are a parent or carer you can consider your role in helping to give babies a good start in life.

1.1 BABIES ARE PEOPLE TOO!

You will have become a student on this course for one or more reasons. You may want to learn more about children out of general interest; you may plan to work towards a formal qualification in the future; or you may have been encouraged to do the course by friends, family or an employer. You may know quite a lot about babies and children through caring for your own or other people's. In this section you will be finding out about very young babies' abilities, and the ways in which they interact with the world around them. To start you off, the following activity asks you to think about some of the commonly held beliefs about babies.

Study note

Throughout *Understanding Children* you will be asked to pause in your reading and undertake an activity, such as the one that follows this note. Activities are not a test, but they are a central way in which distance learning works. They provide an opportunity for you to stop reading and start thinking, working things out for yourself and deciding what you believe. They are a good opportunity for you to take notes on the 'My thoughts' side of your notepad. Remember that your ideas are as important as those in the course materials when you come to write your essays.

ACTIVITY 2 BABIES ARE ...

Allow about 10 minutes

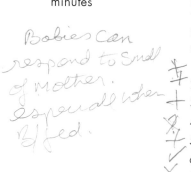

Babies can respond to smell of mother. Especially when B/fed.

For this first activity you should read the following comments about young babies. You may have heard them expressed by friends, colleagues, on the TV or in magazines, or they may be new to you. As you read through the list, tick the ones that you think are probably true, mark a cross by those you disagree with, and put a question mark by any you feel unsure about.

1 Young babies can't feel pain.
2 Babies can't see or hear much when they're newborn.
3 Newborn babies just sleep all day – they don't need much attention.
4 All newborns need is to be clean and well fed.
5 A newborn baby is like a 'blank slate' – it can't think at all.
6 Newborns can express pleasure and displeasure.
7 Newborns can't tell what's going on around them.

COMMENT

How did you get on? In fact the only statement that really deserved a tick is number 6; all the others are either incorrect or very simplified and therefore misleading statements. In number 2, for example, babies' vision has a short range compared with that of an older child, but this enables them to focus on the face of the carer. The limited vision does not prevent babies from interacting or being aware of the world around them. Such beliefs in babies' limited capacity were common among many child development experts in the 1950s, and if parents knew different, they didn't have the authority to challenge them.

These beliefs led to circumstances where babies were treated in ways that would be considered inhumane today. For example, the belief that young babies could not feel pain meant that in the past they were operated on without pain-killing anaesthetic – a practice that would now be considered abusive.

> 'I made sure I cuddled him lots so he got used to me as I was not there all the time once I was released from hospital.'
>
> (parent)

The evidence we will consider later in this section challenges some of these views about babies. While it is true that babies' physical capacities, life experiences and ability to do things without help are limited at this age, it has only been in the last 30 years or so that researchers and others have fully explored just how much very young babies are able to do – that they can express a range of emotions, communicate with adults in quite sophisticated ways, and play a full part in family life. Babies who need to be in incubators after birth are now given frequent contact with their carers, whereas before it was thought that they were 'too young' or 'too ill' to need stimulation and human contact. Severely disabled babies are not routinely now 'left to die' and can develop their own potential. The importance of human contact, love and stimulation for all babies is now well established.

Effective study Developing and demonstrating understanding

Most adult students are trying to fit their studies in between competing commitments – children, work, caring for dependents and family life generally. It is important, therefore, to make sure that the time which you do devote to your studies is time well spent so that you understand what you are studying, rather than just turning the pages!

Have a flick through Unit 1. You will notice that it includes a fair amount of reading, but there are also activities, some of which require you to think and make notes, and others which involve you watching a video recording. Take some time now to think about planning how you will use your time most effectively to work through this unit.

The grid in Table 1 overleaf shows your time divided in to three 'quality' categories of study time: 'high', 'low' and 'parallel' quality. We as authors would characterize each of these as follows:

High: The time when you are able to concentrate best, you read things and they really go in or you find you are able to complete thinking tasks more quickly. This time is likely to be when you are not tired and have few distractions – for some it may be early morning (the larks), for some the middle of the night (the owls). Your alertness, however, is more important than the lack of distractions – just because the middle of the night is the only quiet time in your house does not mean that it is the time when you are buzzing with energy and ideas.

Low: This is when most of us study! It is the time when you are tired and there are many distractions around you. These may be only small chunks of time which do not allow you to really get involved. For the owls it will be trying to get up bleary eyed in the morning and for the larks it will be staying up late dozing over the books.

Parallel: You may or may not use this time at the moment – it is the time when you are doing something which does not occupy your full attention and allows you to think about your studies while you are doing something else. This time can be in many forms – you could be thinking about the course or listening to audio recordings while driving the car, ironing, gardening or cooking. You could be talking or thinking about the course content in social or work situations or even when reading a magazine or watching TV. In the context of *Understanding Children*, you may have sparks of inspiration while spending time with children.

Using the second column from the left of Table 1, try to fill in times in your week which fit into each of the three categories. Leave the other columns for now.

Table 1	Categories of study time				
Quality of time	Time of week	Video/audio activity	Thinking activity	Reading: case study	Reading other
High					
Low					
Parallel					

Handwritten annotations: "9–11" and "Am" in the High row; "2–3" in the Low row, with "Pm", "after lunch", and "Am" handwritten in the Video/audio and Thinking activity columns.

Check whether your grid has too much 'low' quality and not enough 'high' — can you do anything about this? Is there a way in which you could reorganize your week, or get some help from a friend or partner to give you some good-quality time? Studying using only low-quality time will take you longer and be less satisfying.

There are some good jobs to do in low-quality time, though. If you are lucky you may be able to use it just for sorting and ordering your notes, but most people need to make more productive use of their low-quality time. It can be helpful to focus on the parts of your study that you really enjoy as these should keep your attention. Some people also find that 'doing' something — rather than just reading or listening/watching — keeps their attention better, so you might want to save some of the activities for low-quality time.

Did you think of any parallel time that you use now? If not, try to plan this into your week also. Most people think of studying as sitting at a desk reading — but thinking and talking about your subject is just as important. Try keeping a notebook with you to jot down thoughts and observations.

Now fill in the other columns with the parts of the unit you feel you would make best use of your time. You could just tick the kind of task you would aim to do in each category of time, or you could plan in more detail. We have suggested dividing the unit into video/audio activities, thinking activities, reading case study or teaching text material, and finally reading more challenging sections that may contain greater theory or excerpts from other authors.

Save the bits you find hard going for your high-quality time — this might be reading new material or maybe essay writing. Your low-quality time is for less demanding material, although it will be important to choose things which you enjoy and engage you or your mind will drift! Maybe you could focus on sections you have already read. Parallel time is great for audio and video material but also for thinking and talking about new ideas you have come across. Telling a friend or colleague about what you have read is an excellent way of checking out for yourself that you have understood it and practising putting ideas into your own words ready for essay writing.

| **ACTIVITY 3** | WHAT ARE BABIES ABLE TO DO? |

Allow about 30 minutes

The following extract is from a book written by UK child development teachers Carolyn Meggitt and Gerald Sunderland. It summarizes what the majority of babies less than a week old are capable of.

Read through the extract once. Then, using the list of beliefs about babies' limitations from Activity 2 (reproduced here in the margin), write the number beside any statement below which you think disproves it. We have made a start with point (1) for you.

Beliefs about babies

1 Young babies can't feel pain.

2 Babies can't see or hear much when they're newborn.

3 Newborn babies just sleep all day – they don't need much attention.

4 All newborns need is to be clean and well fed.

5 A newborn baby is like a 'blank slate' – it can't think at all.

6 Newborns can express pleasure and displeasure.

7 Newborns can't tell what's going on around them.

they imitate adults.

Sensory development

[This involves eyes, ears, smell, taste and touch.]

Babies:

- will turn their head towards the light and will stare at bright, shiny objects
- are fascinated by human faces and gaze attentively at their carer's face when being fed or cuddled
- open their eyes when held upright
- close their eyes tightly if a pencil of light is shone directly into them
- are known to like looking at high-contrast patterns and shapes
- blink in response to sound or movement
- are startled by sudden noises
- recognise their mother's or main carer's voice, at less than one week old
- cannot hear very soft sounds
- if breastfed, can distinguish the smell of their mother's breasts from those of other women who are breastfeeding
- show a preference for sweet tastes over salty, sour tastes
- (1) are sensitive to textures and to any change of position
- (1) have sensitive skin but may not respond to a very light touch.

Cognitive and language development

[This is to do with thinking, understanding and talking]

Babies:

- are beginning to develop concepts – concepts are abstract ideas, based in the senses and combined with growing understanding [for example, babies become aware of physical sensations such as having an empty stomach, and respond by crying; they also become aware of when they feel full and come to associate that concept with whoever and however they are fed]
- explore using their senses and using their own activity and movement
- make eye contact and cry to indicate need
- respond to high-pitched tones by moving their limbs
- often synchronise actions with the sound of an adult voice
- are often able to imitate, for example copying adults who open their mouth wide or stick out their tongue.

Social Skills in older children

Emotional and social development

[This is sometimes referred to as social skills in older children; it refers to the way in which babies behave with other people]

Babies:

- use total body movements [their whole bodies] to express pleasure at bathtime or when being fed
- enjoy feeding and cuddling
- often imitate facial expressions.

(Meggitt and Sunderland, 2000, pp. 7, 10)

'In his first week I was traumatized and did not notice much. He couldn't see to the best of my knowledge, he hated loud noises and he fed a lot, in fact constantly. He noticed visitors' voices I think and he recognized me very quickly. I don't know if that was the smell of food or what.'

(Mother of 15-month-old boy)

COMMENT

From this extract we can see the range of things babies are capable of. In contrast with the statements you considered in Activity 1, you can see that babies have very sensitive skin, they are startled by sudden noises and they respond to the sight of faces, light and high-contrasting patterns. In fact not only do they have a responsive sense of sight and sound, but they also have a sensitive sense of smell, recognizing their own mother's breast. What is also interesting is that babies are beginning to communicate and interact through facial expressions, noises and movements which are made in response to the actions of other people.

The examples in the extract above are taken from children (most likely white) brought up in UK cultural traditions. In traditions where babies are kept close to the mother all day and can drink milk when they need to, they may hardly cry at all. Eye contact may also not be encouraged.

So far we have been looking at what 'most' or 'typical' babies can do, but just as adults are all different, so are babies. In the next activity, you will read about the experiences of one family responding to the arrival of an individual baby into the world.

MIA'S FIRST BIRTHDAY

It is Mia's first birthday. After a birthday tea and before her bedtime the Family sit down with their photograph albums and watch a video made around the time of her birth. The Family look back to that time and share their experiences of birth and what they noticed she could do.

| ACTIVITY 4 | MIA'S BIRTH |

Allow about 15 minutes

Read the extracts from the accounts by Mia's Family. They were asked to think back to her birth and the few weeks following it, and remember what she was like and how they felt. They used video pictures and photographs to help them.

As you read, use a highlighter pen to mark or make notes on what the Family noticed about Mia and:

- her range of emotions
- her communication and social skills
- her need for contact and her use of her senses

- the things the Family members noticed Mia doing that might make them want to be with her, and to follow her lead in some way.

You will have come across some of these in the reading you did for Activity 3. 'Emotions' refers to Mia's ability to feel happiness, sadness, anger, etc. 'Communication and social skills' will include the way in which she lets other people know what she wants and also how she behaves with other people.

WHEN MIA WAS VERY YOUNG

Ryan:

Mmm – she was very tiny. She stopped crying when Mummy gave her milk. She looked like a ball when she was sleeping. She had funny runny poo. She poked her tongue out at me!

Daisy:

I held her and she snuggled into me and slept. Later she held onto my finger tightly and sucked it. It was the Easter holidays so we were at home when she came from hospital and I spent lots of time with her. I could tell her different cries. She kind of squarked when she was hungry: 'Wah, wah, wah'. When she was uncomfortable the squarks were longer: 'Waahh, waahh, waahh'. When we think she just wanted attention and a cuddle, she would stop crying for a few seconds and then start again.

Jodie:

Mia's birth was very straightforward and we were home the day after she was born. One of the first things I noticed was how much she looked at everything. She stared at toys hanging on her basket, at the faces of adults near her. I think she even saw leaves moving with the wind. I was able to breastfeed her and she would get quite excited when I was getting ready – I swear she could smell what was coming. With so much attention, she seemed to already love being with other people, and Eamon and Daisy could both quieten her unless she was hungry. Our house is so busy and full of people, I think she is going to be the sort of child who enjoys company.

Eamon:

At first I was afraid to hold her in case I was too rough. She seemed so delicate. But it felt so natural once I did. I'll never forget the smell and feel of her skin and hair – really soft. I remember all the different sounds she made – grunts when well fed; snuffles just when dropping off to sleep; the intake of breath before a big cry. She seems to recognize me now and lets me soothe her to sleep after changing her nappy. I was amazed how much of the world she was aware of. She really listens when Daisy is singing – she keeps really still and turns her head to the music. She seems to respond even when Ryan plays his fiddle! It would be lovely if all three of them turn out to be musical.

Figure 13 Ryan playing the violin

Rosalind:

> Mia is a very alert baby. She seemed to like the print on my dress and followed me with her eyes. She already has a strong personality – and a strong grip with her hand!

Michael:

> All the grandchildren are so different. Mia is the seventh and the youngest though there's another one on the way. I noticed how peaceful and contented she seemed to be, and even when she was agitated she was quickly soothed.

Grace:

> What do I remember most? Well, I think she is going to be quite musical. She turned her head when I sang to her and definitely seemed to find lullabies soothing. She loved being carried around so she could see what was going on, and seemed to hate being on her own when she was awake.

COMMENT

Between them, the Family seems to have noticed many areas of Mia's abilities. They observed her expressing a range of emotions, although they had to interpret these as they cannot know exactly what they were – excitement and anticipation; satisfaction; agitation. They noticed her communication and social skills (following Rosalind with her eyes), her pleasure at human contact (snuggling into Daisy, letting Eamon soothe her to sleep), and her use of her senses. Ryan was even able to get Mia to play with him! Some things noted by Mia's Family as being individual to her are in fact very common: copying someone by poking out her tongue, gripping tightly with her finger, responding to the smell of breast milk and to sounds and bright patterns. The fact that Mia does respond in these common ways is important as it helps her to form relationships with her Family as they delight in and respond in turn to her actions.

Some of the observations of Mia are more likely to be individual to her – did you find any of these? We thought her size may be one – it could be that she just seemed small to Ryan, but if Mia really is a small and delicate baby, then her Family may respond to her more cautiously than if she was chubby and robust. Similarly, from the description we have, Mia appears to be quite an emotionally self-sufficient baby – she settles quickly and does not cry for long if she is not hungry or uncomfortable.

The Family is finding Mia rewarding to be with and already are setting up patterns of communicating with her that are quite individual. For example, poking out tongues may become a game that Mia and Ryan particularly enjoy, Eamon and Mia may come to regularly enjoy bedtime routines together, and Rosalind may always greet Mia by holding out her hand and waiting for Mia to grasp it.

'When he was newborn I breastfed on demand and he rarely cried. He let me know he was hungry by "rooting" [open mouth looking for nipple]. By the time he was about three months old he had a "tired" cry which was more of a whinge and an occasional "colic" cry which was more of a shriek!'

(Mother of 17-month-old boy)

Babies differ from each other from a very early age in what they look like and how they behave, and we have seen above that these aspects influence how other people behave towards them. Babies also begin to respond to other people's expectations. People around them may think of a baby in a particular way – as 'calm' or 'strong' or 'serious' or 'musical' – and treat them like this whether or not they actually are. When she turns her head to a song, Mia encourages more songs to be sung and may continue to be thought of and behave like a 'musical' child. If she is thought of as 'small and delicate' by everybody, she may grow used to being protected and may take fewer risks. Sometimes different behaviour is encouraged or discouraged in boys and girls. Researchers at Sussex University in England found adults treated boy and girl babies very differently, depending on whether they thought they were playing with a boy or a girl. The researchers demonstrated this by dressing boy babies in pink and girl babies in blue and observing how adults related to them.

So, the development of babies' personalities comes from the way in which people react to and interpret very common baby behaviours, and also from what the babies are like as individuals and the way in which these characteristics are reinforced (or not) by babies' families and the world around them.

To learn about individual babies and what they can do, it can be useful to watch them and think about the way in which they behave in relation to the people around them.

1.2 WATCHING BABIES

In the next activity you will be introduced to some other babies, all about six months old or younger, who with their mothers are demonstrating some of the things you have read about in the previous section.

Watching babies is a way of getting to know them and what they can do. You can learn a great deal about them by 'standing back' and looking. You can do this with babies you know, but here you will be able to watch a video recording. Baby watching – or observation – can help the ideas that you read about babies come alive. It can help you see a wider range of babies than you might do otherwise, and therefore gain understanding of how different they can be.

Effective study Collecting and using evidence

The ability to learn and gather evidence from real-life observation is an important skill for people working with children, such as nursery teachers, social workers and psychologists. Researchers also use evidence gained from observation to develop their ideas.

Understanding Children is a course which depends upon you being able to observe and think about real children. You may have daily contact with children and will be able to learn a lot from watching and thinking about how they behave and why. The course also includes exercises using video and audio recordings of children, which give you the opportunity to develop your observation skills.

Don't feel that you have to remember everything in the recordings — just like your books they will still be there for you to review. It will help you to make the most of video and audio recordings if you watch/listen for a particular purpose — in other words 'actively'. This is different from the way in which you watch television for leisure, when it is not important whether you learn or think about what you are watching. During any observation:

1   You should try to be alert, concentrating on details.

2   You should aim to be neutral, putting aside expectations and taking note of only what you actually see. Reflecting and making sense of what you observed comes later on.

3   It will be easier to observe if you interact as little as possible with the person you are observing. With young children this can be very difficult, and your behaviour should not make anyone feel uncomfortable.

The next activity will give you an opportunity to practise this as you will be asked to notice particular things as you watch. Thinking of questions about a subject before you watch or listen to recordings — as well as reading books — is a very good way to make sure that you are thinking as well as 'absorbing' information. You may find that watching or listening, as an alternative to reading, is a more effective way for you to learn.

ACTIVITY 5	**VIDEO WATCH**

Allow about 60 minutes

DVD Band 1

For this activity you will be using Band 1 of the DVD, which has a number of short clips of young babies. They are all with their mothers, but babies are just as able to relate to other adults and older children they are close to.

If you can find someone else to share this activity with — a colleague, friend or adult or child family member — it will allow you to share what you found and compare notes. You don't have to meet up; talking on the telephone or by email can be effective too.

As you watch the DVD try to identify and record the facial and body expressions that show how the babies are feeling. You can use the grid provided in Table 2 to record your observations. Put a mark in the correct box for each expression noticed. We have filled in the table for James as an example. You will probably need to watch the DVD band several times to catch everything the babies do.

Expression	**Smile/laugh: happiness**	**Listen/watch**	**Excitement**	**Anticipation**
James	✓	✓		✓
Alice	✓	✓	✓	✓
Sebastian				
David	✓	✓		
Rebecca				

Table 2 Recording babies' expressions of feeling

There is one more part to this activity. Look at the DVD extracts again. For each baby, look for the times when she or he makes the first move in trying to get communication going. This can be by raising a hand, making mouth movements, or making a sound. Put an initial in Table 3 each time they do this, noting whether it's a hand movement (H), mouth movement (M), or with a sound (S).

Table 3 Recording babies' communication

Baby	**Initiates communication**
James	M, H
Alice	
Sebastian	Initiate Smiles anticipates
David	
Rebecca	

COMMENT

Did you find it easy to watch and write at the same time, or did you have to keep playing the extracts over again? It can be hard to concentrate even on a DVD that you can stop and start. Doing two or more things at once — watching, interpreting, maybe counting, then noting down — is quite a complex set of tasks. In real-life observation, there are also many other distractions.

Was it easy for you to identify the different facial or body expressions and to attach emotion to it? Certainly, happiness is quite easy to spot, but what about something like 'anticipation'? Did you think that some babies showed more of one emotion than others?

We noticed how attentive James was, keeping his eyes continually on his mother's face. Alice is very vocal and communicative. Rebecca seemed to be anticipating the toy popping out and got quite excited while waiting. Sebastian makes eye contact and mouth movements to his mother, and David babbles away and initiates frequent conversations.

[Handwritten margin note, left: "I have noticed out how much babies do respond to eing spoken to. It is interesting to note that they can also initiate conversations"]

It was easy to see how the older babies initiated communication. David, for example, was quite vocal and Rebecca was very demonstrative, waving her arms and bouncing up and down. Sometimes it may not be clear that a baby is actually starting off communication, rather than responding to something an adult has started off with them. But did you notice how James, who was only 10 weeks old, raised both hands and made mouthing movements towards the beginning of the clip, and again raised his hand at the end? Although these kinds of movements could be thought of as largely uncontrolled, researchers have found them common and predictable enough to conclude that babies do initiate communication.

An area we didn't ask you to comment on, but is nevertheless important, is the conversations that babies have with their mothers – for example, what Alice's mother was saying when showing her the doll. This kind of talking – where there is exaggerated use of words and syllables and much repetition – is called 'parentese' by child psychologists. It is important in that it introduces babies to the patterns in their language and establishes familiar routines for them.

We hope that by watching the babies on the DVD you have seen just how good they are at interacting with adults, and how much they seem to enjoy doing this.

'Food was his biggest concern so we fed him. I did breastfeed for eight weeks. He was so hungry I was exhausted and had to stop. I suppose we laughed at him a lot and smiled. We cooed and chatted to him a lot.'

(Mother of 15-month-old boy)

1.3 PROMOTING DEVELOPMENT

We hope that after doing the above activity you will be more aware of how babies have the ability to communicate, initiate conversations and show a range of emotions. Adults and other carers have to interpret what babies need, and provide it. We may not always get it right so need to keep an open mind and be able to change our interpretation and our behaviour if required. In addition, without adults or older children to refer to, a baby cannot learn how to get on in his or her own particular family, community and society.

The help babies need is in many forms; as you have seen already, relationships with other people are vital for babies right from the start. They also need to be provided with food and warmth to keep them comfortable, and things to do and think about to help their minds develop. The Family has lots to say about how they help Mia to learn and grow.

[Handwritten note: "A Baby needs to communicate with adults in order to learn and fit in in his own Family, Community & Society"]

ACTIVITY 6 HELPING MIA LEARN AND GROW

Allow about 30 minutes

Read through the comments of Family members. As you read use a highlighter pen to mark examples of where people are helping Mia's development. Then write a brief note of how you think each example might help her. Here they are looking back to when Mia was nine months old.

MIA AT NINE MONTHS

Handwritten margin notes:

① Mia was imitating Daisy by singing.

② She was also showing happiness by kicking and waving her arms around.

③ She showed her displeasure when she was sad by going 'aaah'.

Daisy:

She would sit in her baby chair and we would play games and talk. I would sing her the songs from the Top 20 as well as nursery rhymes. Sometimes she would join in with noises. I knew when she was having fun because she kicked her legs and waved her arms around and laughed. If I stopped singing she would wave and go 'aaah' as if to say 'don't stop'.

Eamon:

Mia is my first child and my first experience of looking after a baby so I wanted it to be right. I hadn't realized how much work it would be getting up in the night – even though Mia slept with us in a baby basket and then in a cot in our room. Being on shift work did mean I saw her at all times of the day and night and she seemed to know that I would be the one to do things for her even in those early months. My favourite time with Mia was and still is breakfast time when she is awake before the others and I spend time playing with her. All of the children are musical – and I can see Mia following in their footsteps. She really listens when Daisy is singing, and even when Ryan plays his fiddle! We eat together and I talk about what we are doing for the day. If I am with her at bedtime, I go over the day very simply and try and piece it together.

Michael:

As I use a wheelchair I became a human pram. I would hold Mia and wheel her around when she was tired or got impatient when waiting for food.

COMMENT

Did you pick out some examples and think of how each might help Mia? Here were our ideas as authors:

1   Daisy sings, laughs and plays with Mia – this interaction will help Mia learn about communicating and taking turns. She is also learning how to develop speech and language and may even have potential as a great musician!

2   Eamon is helping Mia learn important lessons about morning rituals, eating and social skills. She is learning about eating as a social activity and through copying her daddy will eventually learn to eat by herself. She is also learning to stop, take stock and reflect on the day she has had, which is a very useful way of 'letting go' of a day, dealing with stress and learning from your own experience. It is good for improving the memory too!

3   Eamon and Michael are providing Mia with examples of men being carers – an important memory to hold on to as she grows up with images of women caring for babies all around her. She is also learning that wheelchairs are fun and a normal part of her life, which may help her to accept wheelchair users playing a full part in her own and other people's lives.

'Really relaxed, very content! He was not picked up a lot as a baby as I would not let visitors annoy him and I am convinced that it has helped him. I did not let anyone upset me through the pregnancy and it was a good time at work so I think this helped make him relaxed too. His dad is also really relaxed so maybe it's innate!'
(Mother of 15-month-old boy)

Effective study Essay writing

Stop and think for a moment about the situations in which you 'write'. Do you, for example, have to write reports or notes as part of your job? Are you someone who enjoys writing letters or a diary? Or have you embraced electronic technologies and use email and text messages? On the other hand, you may have done very little writing of any kind since you were at school. Whatever your previous experiences of writing, you will find that writing for study has very specific 'rules' or expectations and that writing in a way which you are happy with and which gets the results you want will take practice. The ways in which you write now, along with your past experiences of writing, however, are the starting points for you to begin adapting a style of writing for study.

The kinds of experiences which can influence how you write — and how you feel about writing — include the way in which you learned to write in school, the language or dialect that you use at home and the amount of experience that you have had in reading and writing for study. It can be particularly challenging for students who speak varieties of English or other languages — for example, speakers of regional dialects, Patois or English as a second language — to develop a style of writing which gets good results when studying because the way in which languages like English are spoken is very different from the way in which they are written for study purposes. In addition, people who had difficult, unsupportive or unhappy experiences when learning to write may feel that writing is something which they do not enjoy or feel that they cannot be good at. If any of these experiences apply to you, there is no reason to think that you do not have the ability to be just as good at writing for study as anyone else. Everyone needs to learn the 'rules' and to practise writing, but some have had a head start.

The next activity provides you with an opportunity to practise your writing, and you should continue practising whenever you can — don't wait to be given an activity. If you are worried about your writing or feel that you have had difficult experiences learning to write for study, turn to the activity in the appendix to this unit. This will give you an opportunity to explore the issue further and also talk it over with your tutor.

There are, of course, many ways in which people support babies' development. The extract in the next activity is from the book by Meggitt and Sunderland and lists some of the other ways in which adults and older children can help very young babies to develop their skills. Some babies with physical or mental impairments will respond to these things in different ways, at their own pace.

Different families will have different ways of promoting babies' development according to what they know and can manage. You will see that the extract makes certain class and cultural assumptions — for example, that eye contact is a good thing to encourage, that families will have warm housing so babies can lie without clothes on, and that there is enough money around to choose particular baby-attracting furnishings for the home. Families who are part of some ethnic groups prefer to wrap their babies close to the body, and some may not talk to babies as much as others. The suggestions below will only reflect some traditions of what is helpful and will not be the only ways to help babies develop.

Health warning

Reflecting on your early experiences of learning may have brought back memories or strong feelings. This is quite normal and as you continue with *Understanding Children* you may find that the course materials generate quite strong feelings. If these feelings are uncomfortable or painful you may need to talk to someone about them. You may have a friend or family member who you can talk to but some people find that they would prefer to seek help outside of their families. The Resource Booklet contains a list of organizations that can put you in touch with someone to talk to.

| ACTIVITY 7 | PROMOTING DEVELOPMENT |

Allow about 60 minutes

Read through the text below. There are two tasks to be carried out, each requiring you to write about 200 words.

Promoting development

- Provide plenty of physical contact, and maintain eye contact.
- Massage their body and limbs during or after bathing.
- Talk lovingly to babies and give them the opportunity to respond.
- Pick babies up and talk to them face to face.
- Encourage babies to lie on the floor and kick and experiment safely with movement.
- Provide opportunities for them to feel the freedom of moving without a nappy or clothes on.
- Use bright, contrasting colours in furnishings.
- Feed babies on demand, and talk and sing to them.
- Introduce them to different household noises.
- Provide contact with other adults and children.

(Meggitt and Sunderland, 2000, p.11)

Play

Newborn babies respond to things that they see, hear and feel.
Play might include the following.

- *Pulling faces*
  Try sticking out your tongue and opening your mouth wide – the baby may copy you.
- *Showing objects*
  Try showing the baby brightly coloured woolly pompoms, balloons, shiny objects, and black and white patterns. Hold the object directly

in front of the baby's face, and give the baby time to focus on it. Then slowly move it.

- *Taking turns*
  Talk with babies. If you talk to babies and leave time for a response, you will find that very young babies react, first with a concentrated expression and later with smiles and excited leg kicking.

(Meggitt and Sunderland, 2000, p.11)

Task 1

Think about the reading and then write a paragraph about which points you agree and disagree with, and why. Your paragraph should be about 200 words long. You may disagree with what you read because your experience of bringing up children or being brought up was completely different or because some of the suggestions do not seem practical or comfortable for you to do as an adult. You can write about alternative ways you know of helping babies develop, or things you did from the list that worked for you. This is an opportunity for you to practise writing about your own ideas and experience based upon a piece of reading. Don't spend too much time or worry about the result too much – just have a go.

Task 2

DVD Band 1

Now go back to Band 1 of the DVD and Activity 5. Write a second paragraph of about 200 words describing what the mothers in the DVD did with their babies that appear on the lists of suggestions above.

COMMENT

Many of the items listed in the first section help to give babies a sense of security and being loved, which is good for their ability to form close relationships. These suggestions also help babies' senses to develop and allow them to slowly build up new experiences while in a safe environment. The second set of suggestions can help with their communication skills in listening to language and taking turns to 'talk' and listen and to imitate. The object play can help them get used to some of the different shapes and patterns that will form part of their lives – and which may help them with learning to read later on.

1.4 DIFFERENCE AND YOUNG CHILDREN

Michael, Mia's grandfather, remarked that all his grandchildren were so different from each other, and we looked a little at this earlier in the unit. As authors of this course, we want to cater for the potentially different needs and experiences you have as a student. These experiences can come from a range of origins. For example, the way you approach studying can be to do with your temperament – whether you race through course material or work through it slowly. But it can also be to do with your past experience as a learner – for example, if you were criticized for poor reading in the past, you may lack confidence in your abilities. Babies too are different because of the temperament and personal characteristics they inherit from their families – placidity, seriousness, moodiness. Babies are also different because of the way they interact with and experience the world and people around them once they are born. Some of these differences are even said by researchers to be shaped by what happens in the womb before birth. The expectations placed on them by their families and communities, how they are treated by the adults, siblings and other people who care for them, and the circumstances in which they live, are also very important in shaping who they are. It is a two-way process.

The above discussion relates to an area of interest among academics which is referred to as the 'nature–nurture' debate. Academics and researchers interested in the nature–nurture debate are continually exploring how much of our behaviour and personal characteristics is programmed into us at birth and inherited from others (nature), and how much is a product of how we live our lives and the experiences that we have as we grow (nurture). Most researchers in this area would now accept that people's personalities are not formed by only nature or only nurture, but by a combination of both and the way they interact with each other.

Effective study   Reading for study

When you think of studying, particularly through distance education, you probably think of reading. This section is intended to help you think about and develop your skills in reading for learning.

We assume that you already have some experience of reading or you would not have made it this far into the course. Reading for the purpose of study, however, requires that you develop some new techniques and skills. You will come across further discussion about these techniques as you work through the units of *Understanding Children*. To begin, though, we would like you to spend a few moments thinking about your own experiences so far of reading. Start by reading the following short extract from a book called *Reading at University*.

> What is reading? You may think that this is a foolish question to ask you – because, for example, you've been a reader for so long that it's obvious you know what reading is. Learning to read is one of the first things children do in school and, at a basic level, schools do a good job in teaching most children to read. Nonetheless, the question of what reading is, is not simple. Reading is a complex set of different activities requiring a range of skills. Reflecting on this complexity and on the range of ways in which you can read should help you to become a better reader.
>
> No matter how long ago you learned to read, the ways in which you did so may have influenced both your attitudes to reading and the ways in which you read … We have known many people who, at least partly as a result of unsupportive, unempathic and uninspiring early teaching, find difficulties with reading when they are students. One of the least helpful things that can happen is when a teacher fails to treat children as individuals who differ from one another in their needs as beginning readers.
>
> (Adapted from Fairbairn and Fairbairn, 2001)

What were your thoughts as you read this excerpt? Can you remember your own experiences of learning to read? Your experience is important for you, as it means that you may have your own way of reading which may or may not be helping you with reading for study. Fairbairn and Fairbairn offer examples of a number of reading strategies which, when you begin reading for study, can be unhelpful. Some examples they give are:

- feeling obliged to read every word
- feeling that books should be read in order, without skipping any sections
- reading slowly, sounding out words.

There may be situations when you need to do all of these, but Fairbairn and Fairbairn suggest that they also make your reading for study less effective. Your priorities when reading for study are getting the meaning out of your reading and taking control – so that you decide actively what is important or relevant in a text. This is very different from reading fiction for pleasure when the sounds and experience of the words may be more important than the meaning.

So try taking control of your reading and making active decisions. With practice you will find that you can run your eye over a piece of writing and, through picking up important words, pick up the meaning without needing to 'hear' every word.

Generally we do read books from front to back – in fact this is one of the first lessons children are taught in pre-reading skills – but you can also learn to use the contents page and headings to be selective in which sections you read more closely. You may select according to what interests you, what is relevant to an assignment or maybe skip parts you are already familiar with.

Fairburn and Fairburn are reminding us that reading means different things to different people. Your own feelings about reading are very important and often result from your previous experiences of reading and also how you feel about studying. Before moving on, if you have any concerns about your experiences of learning to read, or reading now, pause to complete the 'reading for study' activity in the appendix to this unit, which will be helpful to share with your tutor.

Communicating need

Daisy could tell the difference between Mia's cries quite soon after birth. Some babies may not communicate their various needs quite so clearly as Mia, and carers have to work hard to interpret them. Carers who can make time to watch, listen and 'be there' for the baby can try different things, asking others if they are not sure. Most babies will tell you if their needs are not being met – by the way they know best: crying!

Below are extracts from accounts of two babies, observed at the time of their birth. They show very different temperaments, and different parental reactions.

> Everyone in the delivery room was struck with how competent and controlled this alert little boy was, moments after birth. His father leaned over, talking to him in one ear. Immediately, Robert seemed to grow still, turning his head to the sound of the voice, his eyes scanning for its source. When he found his father's face, he brightened again as if in recognition … As he was cuddled, Robert turned his body into his father's chest and seemed to lock his legs around one side of his father … By this time, his father was about to burst with pride and delight.

> Chris … was one week overdue. His mother knew [he had] not gained [weight] for the past three weeks, but … no one [had] paid particular attention to her comment, 'He's slowed down' … When he was first born, the nurse and obstetrician were concerned about his colour and lack of response … Assured by the nurse and doctor that he was intact, their hearts nevertheless sank when they saw his wizened face, with ears which protruded … His mother … began to wonder what she had done to her baby … As he lay wrapped in their arms, he looked peaceful enough. But when he was moved even slightly, his face wrinkled up into a frightened animal-looking expression, and he let out a piercing, high pitched wail. They were relieved when the nurses took him away 'to take care of him'.

> (Berry Brazelton and Cramer, 1991, pp. 76–9; reproduced in Oates (ed), 1994, pp. 201–3)

These extracts are of course selective, and don't show the whole picture of the babies' births or what happened afterwards. But they provide powerful accounts of these babies' experiences of birth and the world. They also illustrate how the babies reacted to it at this early stage, and how these reactions had a deep effect on the adults around them and their relationships with the baby.

Although we cannot know exactly what he felt, the account of Chris gives an impression of how miserable and frightened he must have felt, as well as lacking in energy. The hospital's delay in intervening to deliver him when his mother thought something was wrong and the guilt she seemed to feel at his condition when he was born will take time to work through. Chris's experience of the world so far is of something that is alarming and not a safe place. You can see his parents reacting anxiously to him, his appearance of vulnerability and his unsettled behaviour.

On the other hand, Robert doesn't seem worried by the world he has come in to and immediately settles into relationships with his parents and taking an interest in the world around him. This has a reassuring and rewarding effect on his parents and others who meet him.

In case you are wondering if babies like Chris can be damaged by their experiences in hospital, there is some reassuring evidence from a television programme that this is not necessarily the case. A baby who had spent quite a bit of time in an incubator after birth was encouraged to visit the hospital at around two years old to see if it brought back unpleasant memories. It didn't. Of course, it's too simple to draw firm conclusions from this, and the parents had loved and supported the child continually through his experience. But it's worth bearing in mind that early experiences can be compensated for.

Responding to need

How adults react to babies' needs will depend on a number of things. These include how relaxed they feel about being a carer and what they have learned from their own childhood about caring for babies. It also includes what is considered to be good childcare practice at the time, wider cultural expectations about bringing up children, and their particular feelings and relationship with the baby in question. A mother or father who has an idea of how they think babies ought to behave and what their baby will be like – for example, that the baby will sleep through the night and will quickly take to breastfeeding – may be disappointed if their baby does not do these things. They may think it's something they are doing 'wrong' and their feelings will affect how they treat the baby. Sometimes adults put their own interpretations on baby behaviour. For example, a baby who cries when it's hungry but doesn't get food quickly enough may cry louder and harder. This may irritate its carer who thinks the baby is being 'naughty' and may keep the food away for longer to try to 'teach' the baby to wait. But the baby doesn't understand what's happening – he or she just wants hunger satisfied and to have attention, so continues to cry. This shows that carers can get into patterns of behaviour with babies that are unhelpful to both sides.

1.5 DIFFERENT BABIES, DIFFERENT FAMILIES

In the first part of the unit we learned that babies can do more than adults think, despite having not been in the world for long. We then looked at how adults and older children can help babies learn and develop. What the extracts above show is that:

- babies' temperament
- how they experience the world
- how they behave towards other humans and
- how humans behave towards them

all matter, and that babies are a product of them all.

The next activity gives you a chance to think about different babies and their different and similar needs. We also look at the different expectations carers have of babies, and what this might mean for the babies while they grow up.

DIFFERENT BABIES, DIFFERENT FAMILIES

On the same day that Mia was born, ten other babies were born in the hospital. Two of them were in the room with Mia and Jodie, and Jodie got to know the families while they were there. She collected accounts from them.

| ACTIVITY 8 | BABIES ARE DIFFERENT |

Allow about 40 minutes

Read through the accounts of each baby, and think about the following questions. We have also included the accounts of Mia from earlier. Record your thoughts on the chart in Table 4.

- What individual characteristics do you think each baby has?
- What hopes, expectations and concerns do the parents express about their baby?
- What you think each baby needs from its carers? Are there any differences between Mia, Tembi and Harish?
- Are there differences in the way Mia, as a girl, and the boys are talked about in the accounts below?

We have filled in some points for Mia to get you started, but you may want to add more.

Table 4   How the babies are different

Baby	What baby is like	What family expect	What baby needs
Mia	Tiny, delicate, good at communicating, happy, alert, contented, musical	She will be musical, She will be sociable and enjoy company	Love, attention, time to play, feeding and keeping clean
Harish			
Tembi			

Mia

Jodie:

> Mia's birth was very straightforward and we were home the day after she was born. One of the first things I noticed was how much she looked at everything. She stared at toys hanging on her basket, at the faces of adults near her. I think she even saw leaves moving with the wind. I was able to breastfeed her and she would get quite excited when I was getting ready – I swear she could smell what was coming. With so much attention, she seems to already love being with other people and Eamon and Daisy can both quieten her unless she is hungry. Our house is so busy and full of people, I think she is going to be the sort of child who enjoys company.

Eamon:

> At first I was afraid to hold her in case I was too rough. She seemed so delicate. But it felt so natural once I did. I'll never forget the smell and feel of her skin and hair – really soft. I remember all the different sounds she made – grunts when well fed; snuffles just when dropping off to sleep; the intake of breath before a big cry. She seems to recognize me now and lets me soothe her to sleep after changing her nappy. I was amazed how much of the world she was aware of. She really listens when Daisy is singing – she keeps really still and turns her head to the music. She seems to respond even when Ryan plays his fiddle! It would be lovely if all three of them turn out to be musical.

Harish

Harish is the first-born child of Meera and Jonathan. Meera is a general practitioner in a village practice and Jonathan is self-employed as an architect. Meera is an only child but her parents are from large families and all live quite close by. Harish will have many relatives to get to know. Jonathan's family live in Scotland, where he has five sisters and brothers all living reasonably close to each other. Harish is the youngest of ten grandchildren to his family in Scotland, but the first to his family in England.

Meera:

> Harish was born by Caesarian in the end. I was determined to have him with me and breastfeed him from the start rather than let the nurses bottle-feed him to allow me to rest. It was tiring but not hard. He drank milk frequently and cried loudly when he was hungry, being changed and being washed. In between he slept and was very alert when awake, though we know now that he has only limited hearing, which we are still trying to get used to. We have busy lives and travel a lot and want him to come with us and to do all the things we do and get a good experience of the world. We are not planning to have more children so he will need to rely on his own company and just ours when at home. But he will have a big social

Figure 14 Harish, Meera and Jonathan

Figure 15 Tembi and Safiya

life with his grandparents and other relatives. My parents have waited so long for a grandchild!

Jonathan:

I want to play an equal part to Meera in Harish's life, and my work will allow this. He seems to be at ease with both of us, though Meera has the advantage of the food supply! Meera has to take it easy for a few weeks which means I can take Harish out in the baby sling and already he seems to notice so much around him. I would love it if he took an interest in the countryside, buildings and the world around. I know it's silly but I look at his fingers and think he will make a good craftsperson or artist. As the youngest grandchild on my side of the family, he will have to compete. But he will also get wonderfully spoiled!

Tembi

Tembi is the first-born child of Safiya and Abena. Safiya is a community worker and Abena is studying to be a veterinary surgeon. Tembi will have grandparents and other relatives in London from Safiya's family, and Abena's father is in Liverpool. The couple are active in the local lesbian community and also jointly co-ordinate a group for African women. Tembi has a sperm-donor father.

Safiya:

It took us years to find the right donor for me, and for it to finally work. So we have invested a lot in having Tembi in more ways than one. And he certainly came out angry! He hasn't settled well at all and it takes the two of us to calm him down if he's upset. We are thinking of buying him a dummy, would you believe! We want him to be proud of having two mums but we know he will have to put up with other people's prejudices. He will know quite a few children of lesbians though, which will help. We also plan to share his care with a childminder so we can both have time for work and study.

Abena:

We want Tembi to know he has a right to be here – and he definitely lets us know that he's here! He has a huge appetite, little need for sleep and seems to want constant attention. When he gets it he's very rewarding – looks at us, grabs our hair and is quiet for a while. I think he is going to be very clever – he already looks and tries to grab things and we have put lots of moving toys above his basket so he can watch them.

COMMENT

How did you get on? Did you find many differences between the babies?

We noted that all the babies needed attention, comfort, food, shelter, to be touched, and somewhere to sleep peacefully.

We also noticed some differences. Mia is perceived as 'delicate' and Harish is described as protesting loudly when he is hungry or uncomfortable. Tembi comes over as quite demanding and robust. There are often differences in the way babies are described because of their gender. For example, 'tiny' and 'peaceful' are often used to describe girls whereas a boy might be described more neutrally as 'small' or 'quiet'. Girls are less likely to be described as 'robust' or 'protesting loudly' as angry or noisy behaviour is generally not encouraged in girls.

One reader commented how she really identified with the mothers of Tembi: 'My son had so much energy he wore me out. The only way I managed was to have as many people as possible to share his care with me. Luckily, he didn't mind and has grown up to be a really sociable four-year-old.'

All of the families have expectations that their babies will be able to 'fit in' with established lifestyles, and this may be more or less difficult depending upon each baby's personality and the particular expectations. Harish, as a baby who quickly expresses discomfort, may find travelling and changes in routine difficult. He may also experience negative reactions to his hearing impairment. Tembi's robust character may help him to forge a strong identity if, as his family fear, he does face prejudice due to being the son of a black lesbian couple. For all of these babies, the development of their personalities will be as a result of a combination of the characteristics that they are born with and the way in which people around respond to them.

1.6 CONCLUSION

Young babies can do more than we often give them credit for. From birth they are active participants in life, making sense of their worlds and influencing them.

In this, they need other people to help them, and other children and relatives can play a big part in their lives. Through Mia and her Family's experience of her birth, you have seen the significance of other people to her. You have also been introduced to two other families with babies the same age as Mia. They live in different circumstances and have different expectations of babies. As the families grow up together, they will have to balance and probably adapt these expectations with the reality of living together.

In the next section, we focus on learning about one area babies can't do without – secure relationships with other people.

Key points

- Research has shown that very young babies can communicate, feel and do much more than was believed in the past.

- Babies benefit from close, predictable and responsive relationships with other people.

2   SECURE RELATIONSHIPS

CORE QUESTIONS

- How important are close relationships to babies?
- What do babies and toddlers get from having a range of relationships?

Figure 16 Mia with her main carers

In this section you will find out why early secure relationships are important to babies and young children. These secure relationships do not have to be only with the mother or father. Some babies have closer relationships with adults other than their parents or older children. What is important is that babies are close to one or more people who are consistently around and that these are good quality relationships. The consistency and quality of the emotional relationship is more important than the biological relationship.

You will be introduced to two babies whose experiences of early relationships were not straightforward, but who are both growing up well. Through looking at video extracts of their lives, we will discuss what babies need from close relationships and how these relationships can be fostered.

2.1 THE VALUE OF CLOSE RELATIONSHIPS

Humans are social beings. We usually live together in groups, eat together, play together and work together. We depend on other people to supply our food, clothing and home services. To survive we therefore have to build relationships of different kinds. Some are more businesslike, others more personal.

For babies and young children, relationships begin with the personal kind and are usually with members of their family. Child psychologists who study these relationships have concluded that the quality of them is important for children's future emotional well-being. If relationships are secure, the child is able to trust that others will protect them when they do not feel safe; this then gives them the confidence and ability to explore the world around them.

In this course we are using the term 'close relationships'; you may have also come across the term 'attachments' to refer to the close, two-way emotional relationships between children and caregivers.

DAISY'S EARLY MEMORIES

Daisy remembers a close relationship. This is what she wrote:

It is my dad, Graham, who was closest to me when I was little. He was working nearby when I was born and mum went back to work full-time when I was six months old. Dad used to get up to me in the night, take me to and from the childminder and do all that kind of thing. I remember sitting in my baby car-seat singing with him, getting lost in the supermarket and being so pleased to see him …

Some children have secure relationships with a daycare worker, foster carer, close friend or relative, or an older sister or brother. It does not have to be a biological parent. It is through the relationships they have with other people – both good and bad – that babies and children learn about themselves: who they are and what they can and cannot achieve.

ACTIVITY 9 — BEHIND RELATIONSHIPS

Allow about 40 minutes

DVD Band 2

Watch DVD Band 2. You will need to watch it more than once to get a feel of who is in it and the points about relationships being illustrated. Then watch it again, specifically to answer the following questions. Make a note of your answers.

- What reasons were given for why Charlotte may not have formed a close relationship with her mother?
- How did Charlotte behave that made the narrators comment that things were not right between her and her mother at that time?
- How could these early experiences be said to have affected their relationship now Charlotte is two?

COMMENT

We learned that for much of the time Charlotte was a baby, her parents were separating from their marriage and that the children were frequently moved between the two parents. Charlotte's mum, Emma, acknowledges that it must have been a difficult time for Charlotte, as it was for all of them.

We are alerted to the fact that all might not be right in the relationship by Charlotte's taking part in something called the 'strange situation test'. During this test babies' reactions are observed when their main carer leaves them in an unfamiliar place for a short while. Charlotte's reaction was to seem unconcerned when Emma left the room and also when she returned. At one point she did acknowledge Emma had returned by moving closer to her, but then stopped. This was interpreted by the child psychologist watching to mean that Charlotte was unsure of her relationship with Emma. The narrator said she was 'not sure if her mother loves her'. The baby who was said to have a secure relationship with the mother had been unhappy to see her leave and pleased to see her return.

Did you notice, though, how hurt Emma was with the feedback about their relationship? She had known things were bad, but had no idea of their effect on Charlotte. She had thought Charlotte too young to remember the moving and the break-up of the marriage. As she says, she 'loves Charlotte to pieces'.

By the time Charlotte is two years old, Emma acknowledges that they have difficulties and that Charlotte in her words is 'strong-willed', 'won't listen' and has an 'attitude problem'. Emma is not sure what to do next. She also acknowledges that, if she could go back in time, she would not have chosen to have two children at the time she did.

What the account shows is that people's lack of readiness to be parents and stressful circumstances surrounding their lives can influence the relationships they have with their children. It also shows that having feedback on the effects on children, while being distressing, can be helpful, as parents will almost certainly not want their children harmed.

Postscript

What is learned from watching the whole video featuring Charlotte is that for two years the family went through a great deal of change. Charlotte, her mum and her brother lived in temporary accommodation and were very unsettled. The children did not see their father often and relations were strained between the parents. However, around the time Charlotte was two, the family moved into more secure accommodation. Charlotte and her mother also had help from a play therapist, who worked with them to build their relationship. Charlotte's mother was very receptive to change and the support seemed to work well. What this demonstrates is that poor relationships can change for the better. The narrator of the programme concludes that making everyday experiences positive for children can offset a shaky start and that even if people have wretched childhoods they can be 'turned around'.

Where knowledge comes from – points to think about

The 'strange situation test' has been used by child psychologists in Western Europe and the United States for many years to assess the quality of attachment relationships in young children. This had usually been done with mothers as the main carers. What it did do for Charlotte's mother was to allow a discussion to take place about her relationship with Charlotte. This then enabled change to happen.

The majority of research on early relationships used as a source of expertise in the UK comes from studies carried out by Western European and American researchers, using children from their own cultural groups. This is now changing, but it means that we cannot generalize this work across countries and cultures. Secure relationships may be universally needed by babies and have been found by researchers to exist across cultures, but some of the interpretations of what secure relationships should be like are very specific to European-American cultures. For example, another test of babies' secure attachment looks at how much they explore their surroundings and show curiosity when in a 'strange situation' with their mother present. But there are societies and ethnic/cultural groups where babies are not encouraged to explore, play away from family or show curiosity, so would not behave in this way when young (Cole, 1998, p. 28). In assessments of the security of their relationships, therefore, these babies may be wrongly assessed as being not secure. These babies would also not be at a disadvantage in their society when they are older, but might be in the UK. Much depends on the context and which behaviours are valued and promoted.

Research has shown that even if a close relationship is not with a child's parents, as long as a child has someone who is consistently 'there' for them, they are likely to be OK:

> it should never be considered to be 'too late' for any child to be offered the opportunity to experience a good relationship with an adult who considers them to be special.

(Daniel, Wassel and Gilligan, 1999, p. 38)

This is the role that foster carers, childminders and daycare workers sometimes have with young children. Some adults will have had experiences that make it hard for them to live up to expectations of 'good' parenting. They may lack confidence; they may have had a poor experience of being parented themselves so don't know what to do; they may not feel ready to be a parent; or they may not want to have a child.

Research has also shown that children can put up with more than professional childcare workers often think they can – even what some might describe as neglect – as long as their caregiver is predictable. Inconsistency and unpredictability in a relationship can make a child feel very insecure. The early experiences of attachment that children have, then, influence how they think about and respond to other relationships.

'Oliver's most important people are myself and my husband but he realizes that we do different things. He is more likely to bring me a book whereas he is more likely to take a box to my husband to put on his head for a silly game. I still breastfeed twice daily so at these times I'm definitely the most important! He doesn't have any friends that he repeatedly chooses to play with yet but his "Tigger" and "Truffles the dog" seem important to him!'
(Mother of 17-month-old boy)

ACTIVITY 10	IMPORTANT RELATIONSHIPS

Allow about 20 minutes

For this activity, look at the picture below which shows the range of different people our case study Family members feel or felt close to when they were young. Each person in Mia's Family has thought of the people they were close to in their first few years of life. Count up the different types of people (e.g. mother, uncle) represented in their lists overall.

Do you notice anything about the range or type of people mentioned?

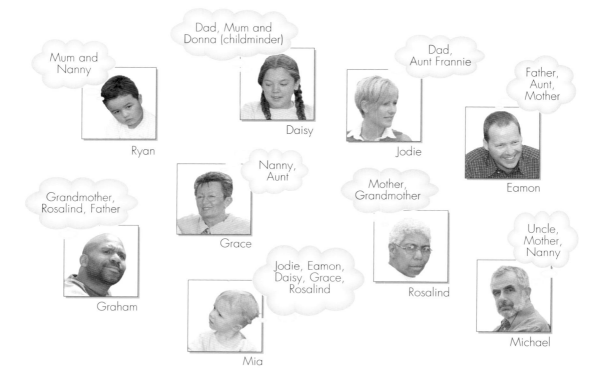

Figure 17 Who each member of the family feels or felt close to

COMMENT

We counted 10 different types of people. These were mother, father, aunt, uncle, sister, grandmother, grandfather, great aunt, nanny, childminder. You may have been surprised at the number of people who were involved and were not the mothers.

FAMILY RELATIONSHIPS

Commenting on the list, Daisy observed:

> When Dad and Mum separated I cried and cried even though I was glad that there would be no more arguing. I could sometimes hear them at night – I used to creep down and sit on the stairs to listen. I didn't like it and was always scared about what might happen.
>
> I missed Dad loads when he moved out but we spoke lots on the telephone and at first he lived near so I saw him almost every day. It helped that Mum and Dad both talked to me and said that splitting up was nothing I had done, just them.
>
> Mia used to cry when I went to school but Mum and Grace said she was fine a few minutes later. I always get big hugs and smiles when I get home.

Graham said:

> My Mum was very ill when I was born and died when I was six months old. I lived with Dad and Rosalind his sister – they both brought me up till I was six and Dad died. Rosalind has had to be both parents to me.

Jodie explained the people she chose:

> Dad always worked from home. He is disabled and a wheelchair user and it was very easy for him to be around after I was born, and for my three brothers who came after me. Aunt Frannie is Dad's sister and was a nurse. She lived with us until I was eight and then went to Argentina to do nursing. Mum worked very long hours and I loved being with her when she was around, but she wasn't 'there' for us much – I remember her being worn out most of the time.

In the next activity, you will again look at close relationships within a family through another video extract. Jamie is also featured in the BBC series 'Child of Our Time'. He lives with both parents and has an older sister and brother.

Effective study Evaluating ideas

Academic study is rarely just about describing or reproducing what you have read; it is more often about people presenting different views about a subject and engaging in logical, evidence-based argument. If everybody agreed and your job was just to reproduce facts, then subjects would become very dull!

As you move through your studies you will often come across the word 'argument', particularly in assignment guidelines. It is important, therefore, that you understand what it means in the context of writing your essays. One way of looking at the meaning of argument is to break it up into three stages:

- First, your essay needs to present more than one point of view.

- Secondly, you need to use evidence from these views to build a case – think of a lawyer gathering evidence in a court hearing.

- Finally, you need to come to a conclusion – in other words be judge as well as lawyer. Having presented and thought about all of the evidence, what do you think? This is sometimes called 'taking a position' on a subject.

It is for this reason that, although you need to learn about what other people have said, you are also encouraged from the start to note down your own opinions – it is from such ideas and observations that great revolutionary ideas grow. You are not expected to be able to develop such arguments in your essays right now – just like reading for study and essay writing, it takes practice. However, engaging in debate may be one of the main differences between the kind of study you may have experienced in school and higher education. It can also be exciting and rewarding as you begin to feel that you can join in with arguments about interesting subjects.

In this part of the unit you will encounter one argument about close relationships, or 'attachment'. Although attachment is a well-established concept, since it was first identified as being important for children in the 1950s there have been debates about:

- whether babies need just one carer, who should ideally be the mother
- whether babies who do not have a secure attachment in their first two years are permanently damaged psychologically and emotionally.

As you work through Activities 11 and 12 and the discussion related to them, try to decide what you think about these arguments. Keep a page in your notes with these questions written down, and use them to jot down your ideas, relevant experiences and most importantly any evidence that you come across to support either view.

ACTIVITY 11   OBSERVING RELATIONSHIPS

Allow about 45 minutes

DVD Band 3

Watch DVD Band 3, which shows Jamie and his family from when Jamie was born to now he is about two years old. You will need to watch it through a few times to become familiar with it.

Now watch it again and write answers to the following.

- What did Jamie's mother say about the background to Jamie's birth and what happened after the birth?
- How are we led to believe this has affected the relationship between Jamie and his mother?
- What points are being made in the extract to show that difficulties with this early relationship have been overcome?

COMMENT

Jamie's mother is very open about the fact that she had not wanted another child, that she had been sterilized and it had not worked. She had been the full-time carer but had also been severely depressed after Jamie was born, and Jamie had in her words not been 'an easy baby'. Fortunately, she had access to a car and had found a way of managing her depression to some extent by driving around with Jamie. However, all these things made it hard for her to 'bond' with him and as a result she feels their relationship is not close.

One of the differences between Jamie's and Charlotte's situations is that Jamie has a father who is living at home and is more available to make a relationship with him. The film makes the point that babies need love and affection or they become insecure, so they will look for this source of love and 'head for it', which is what Jamie did. Jamie is more attached to his father and his affection is returned. Jamie's family scored the highest in a happiness test the parents took. This is particularly good to know when you think of how the pregnancy and birth started out.

In Europe and North America in the 1950s and the twenty or so years afterwards, women who found it hard to make relationships with their babies from birth were made to feel they had 'failed' as mothers and that their babies would suffer as a result. This view was promoted by government departments and childcare professionals and based on the work of child psychologists such as John Bowlby. This focus on the importance of the mother ignored other close relationships the child might have. The video extract you have just watched is an example of how mothers need not be the closest person a young child relates to.

2.2 PROMOTING CLOSE RELATIONSHIPS

In the video extracts and throughout the course so far you have become aware of some of the ways parents can help their child have secure relationships:

- tuning into and anticipating what they need
- giving them food and drink when they need it
- letting them sleep when tired
- giving them attention
- being predictable
- giving them love and security.

In the next section you will see what Mia and the children who were born at the same time have experienced.

RELATIONSHIPS IN DIFFERENT FAMILIES

Daisy is interested in finding out how Harish's and Tembi's experiences might be similar to or different from Mia's. Being involved with Mia has been Daisy's first opportunity to really find out about babies and what it is like to look after them – she does not remember much about Ryan when he was a baby. The families have stayed in touch since the birth of the three babies, and as their first birthdays approach Daisy spends some time observing Harish and Tembi with one of their carers.

Allow about 30 minutes

Read the case study material below about each child. Identify what the carers seem to be doing to build secure and close relationships with the child.

BUILDING CLOSE RELATIONSHIPS

Daisy on Harish:

I watched Harish with his dad getting dressed after a bath and having a bedtime story. He can't hear very well so his dad was teaching him to use sign language while he spoke to him and they had to look at each other all the time. They were both paying lots of attention to each other. They played 'peep-bo' with the towel and had a laugh. When Harish didn't want to clean his teeth his dad made a game out of it and he did it. Later his dad read him a story, signing some of the words and getting him to sign them back. They looked really happy together.

Daisy on Tembi:

Tembi goes to a childminder, Eunike, two days a week and I was allowed to visit him there. He was having lunch and eating by himself in a very messy way. But he was having fun. Eunike seemed to really like him. After lunch they went out in the garden and played ball with some older children. Tembi got scared of an aeroplane flying low but Eunike gave him a hug and held him till it had gone past.

Daisy on Mia:

Mia was at Grandma's and Grandpa's home. They were in the garden and Mia was with Grandpa putting food out for the birds. She was sitting on his lap in the wheelchair. Grandpa would talk to her all the time and say the name of the birds that might come. Mia was saying 'bir, bir' and waving at the sky.

COMMENT

Did you find it easy to identify positive behaviour? Certainly all the children seemed happy and secure with their carers. There didn't seem much evidence of insecure behaviour. Tembi came nearest to feeling insecure when the low-flying aeroplane came past but he was quickly comforted by Eunike. All the babies are likely to have been smiling, another expression of secure relationships, as they are clearly having a good time.

We picked out the following ways the carers were helping:

* paying close attention
* doing things together
* comforting when scared
* praising and watching fondly
* playing games
* laughing together.

The very minimum that a baby needs in order to form a secure relationship is to have a person reliably and consistently there to meet their needs. As you can see from Daisy's observations, carers can do much more than this to encourage a strong bond. One of the most important of these is being responsive to the baby – reacting to the baby's communication in a way in which shows them that you are involved and 'tuned in' to them. This is sometimes called 'attentive behaviour', and contrasts with behaviour which is consistently 'inattentive'. This inattentive or neglecting behaviour, even where the physical care of a baby is good, can be damaging for babies and young children as they are not able to really 'connect' with another human being.

Did you notice also that a range of carers was involved – a father, grandfather and childminder? It's important to remember that people other than a child's biological parents can provide good quality attachments for a child. We will look at these other people in the next section.

2.3 IMPORTANT OTHERS

Parents and immediate family are naturally important to young children. Other adults – such as childminders and family friends – and children are too, but don't always get the credit they deserve for their part in children's lives. Yet we see from the pleasure Mia gets from them that these other relationships are important and should be encouraged.

Fathers, mothers and others

In the previous section we looked at the range of people a young child can be close to. In this section, we concentrate on particular kinds of 'others': those grandparents, childminders and daycare workers who can share substantial amounts of care with the young child's parents, and the other children – sisters and brothers, friends and neighbours who form part of a child's social life.

Figure 18 Mia with important others

IMPORTANT OTHERS

When the children were 18 months old, Daisy carried out a piece of research for a school project to find out how many people Mia, Harish and Tembi knew. She describes what she did:

Mum had kept in touch with the other mums, and we had got to know the families a little so I was able to visit them and do this work. I asked my best friend Sammy to do the work with me. I wanted to ask the children who their special adults and children were and I knew that some of them might not be able to tell me. Sammy and I decided to use photos and to spend two days with each child during the summer holidays, taking photos of where they went and who they played with. We already had lots of Mia, but not of all the things she did. We used throw-away cameras with each family. We also took a tape recorder to record what we did with the children.

Each child was very busy on the days we were there. We picked a weekday and a weekend day for each, when they were with other people.

When we had all the photos we picked out the best ones and kept them to show the babies when we saw them next.

Daisy continues:

We went back one more time to visit the children and to stick the photos on the sheets with them. We picked up a photo and asked the baby which people were in the photo and where it should go. Harish's childminder and father helped us to understand Harish.

All the children could name quite a few people in the pictures and Mia and Harish were able to say things like 'play', 'swings', 'car' when asked what they were doing with certain people. They got quite excited looking at the pictures and Tembi even kissed the one of Eunike!

Table 5 The chart Daisy and Sammy filled in for each child

Child	Weekday adults	Weekday children	Weekend adults	Weekend children
Mia	Jodie, Graham, Rosalind, Grace and Michael	Daisy and Ryan	Graham, Jodie Eamon	Daisy and Ryan
Tembi	Safia, Abena, Eunike	Eunike's two daughters and another little boy being minded	Safia, Abena, Safia's parents and brothers and sisters	Roberta, Lilly and Twame (Tembi's cousins)
Harish	Meera, Jonathan		Meera, Jonathan, Meera's parents, Meera's brothers and sisters	

We hope this section has shown that children at this age can have a range of relationships. But you might be worried that too many people might be confusing and overwhelming to such young children, and that things have gone from one extreme to another in childcare. First, there was only the mother; now there are so many people it's hard to keep up with them. So, can children manage? The next section considers this.

2.4 MANAGING RELATIONSHIPS

In the 1950s messages about a young child needing their mother as a full-time carer were being promoted by child-development specialists in the UK and used by the government of the time to encourage women who had worked in the Second World War to return to full-time mothering. From the same sources came messages that children might get confused if they had more than one carer – that they wouldn't know who their mother was if they had to go to a childminder, or might not be able to handle different caring styles. It took time for research to filter through that demonstrated that, provided there are one or several carers with whom a child has a close relationship, young children can manage differences in style and a range of different carer relationships. Ideally, the adults involved need to talk frequently with each other about the care they provide, to check they are all working together in what's best for a child.

RELATIONSHIPS WITH CARERS

Mia has five main daytime carers, plus Rosalind once a week. How does she manage to adapt to the different caring styles and settings?

Daisy comments:

Mum works from home a lot but has to go to meetings on the same two mornings a week and on those days Mia goes to Grandma and Grandpa. If I say to her 'Grandma and Grandpa today' she says 'Yay!' and goes to the cupboard to get the bag she always takes there. Rosalind takes her to an older person's lunch and social club on a Friday afternoon and if we ask her what she is going to do with Rosalind she says 'Din-din, play'. At other times, Eamon has her in the mornings when he is on night shift and sleeps in the afternoon when Mum takes over. I do things with her when I first come home from school – we have tea together and I take her out for a walk. When I come in, she rushes to the cupboard and looks for her favourite drinking mug.

Michael remarks:

I'm amazed at how adaptable Mia is. Even if she is not feeling well and would rather be at home, she seems to know that she'll be staying here till the cat comes in and demands food! Our house is quite small and cramped, and has lots of ornaments on surfaces. Mia learned quickly that she couldn't run around in every room and asks to go outside when she wants to run. We are also much quieter here, whereas at home everyone talks at once and there's lots of noise. She just fits in quite naturally.

Jodie:

I wasn't sure how Mia would cope with what I think is a fragmented week but she does seem to be doing just fine. We are careful to try and have a set routine during the week and to talk about where she is going at the beginning of each day. Even when things go wrong she wouldn't have to go with strangers and she knows so many of Rosalind's friends there would always be back up in an emergency.

| ACTIVITY 13 | HOW MIA ADAPTS |

Allow about 15 minutes

Re-read the above accounts and note down:

- the changes Mia has to adapt to when she is with different carers
- how she lets people know she is aware of the different routines and happy to be doing them, and
- how the adults try to make sure she is not confused and feels secure in what she does.

COMMENT

Even before she is two years old, Mia seems to be very much in control of her social world. If given a clue, she knows where she is going on particular days, with whom, and what to expect. She anticipates what she will be doing and looks forward to it. She lets people know she understands that she is going to her grandparents' houses by getting the bag she usually takes there. She also lets them know that she is pleased to be going. At her regular lunch-club appointment with Rosalind, she again clearly knows what she does there and enjoys it. With Daisy, she associates her coming in from school with having tea together. Different people bring different experiences to Mia, and she seems to like the variety. The adults remark on how adaptable she is, fitting into a quiet lifestyle or a smaller home. All her carers seem to make a point of telling her what she is doing on that day – keeping her informed all the way through, which can be a great help in her being able to feel in control of her life.

Mia may be unusual in that all her main carers know each other well, most being part of her wider family. Other children's carers may know just one parent and any children who are sisters and brothers, and may also be unlikely to know grandparents and other relatives. The case study above is not necessarily suggesting that this is the only good practice, but is illustrating particular points.

UNIT 1 **BABIES BEING HEARD**

2.5 CONCLUSION

We hope that, through this course so far, you have learned about young babies' abilities and about the range of relationships they are able to handle, provided they have a few close people who give them unconditional love. We hope also that you will see how important the wider family can be in sharing the care of children. Not everyone is fortunate enough to have family living nearby who have the time to share the care, or who get on well enough with them to be able to rely on them in this way. Note also the big part that Daisy plays in Mia's life.

There's an African proverb that says 'it takes a village to raise a child'. Although we don't have the village-type set-up in our case study Family, we do know that bringing up children can be a collective responsibility, and if it is, everyone benefits from making a difference to a child's life, and also their own.

Key points

- Although close, predictable relationships are very important in helping children grow up into secure and confident young people, broken or lost attachments do not necessarily result in permanent harm.

- Contrary to the belief that babies should only have one carer, as long as their carers are predictable and responsive, babies can benefit from a range of relationships.

Effective study   Reflection

In the following exercise you will be asked to do some 'reflection' through reviewing your progress in effective study so far. This is important as part of your assignments will be a reflection on your development in the areas of *effective study*.

'Reflection' is a term which you are likely to come across a fair amount and you may find that it refers to the process of 'reflecting' on different things. This can be confusing.

In simple terms the word 'reflection' means to think about something. If you find the idea of writing about your thoughts off-putting, you are not alone! Many people feel uncomfortable about talking and writing about themselves.

One way to think about writing your reflections is to see your own thoughts, ideas and memories as your source of evidence. So, just as when you use sources of evidence such as quotes from course materials in essays, your reflective writing will use examples of your ideas of experiences.

The *effective study* sections will look at three kinds of reflection.

- The first relates to thinking about how you are studying and learning.
- In Unit 2 you will read about reflecting upon what you study.
- In Unit 3 you will reflect by using your experience of the topic (children) in an essay.

At the end of each unit you will find a review activity intended to help you practise reflecting on your progress in studying effectively. Your answer to this activity should be completed on a separate piece of paper and handed in as part A of each assignment. You will find further guidance in your Assignment Booklet. Here is your first opportunity.

| ACTIVITY 14 | EFFECTIVE STUDY REVIEW ACTIVITY |

Allow about 15 minutes

Complete this activity on a separate piece of paper and send it to your tutor as part A of assignment 1.

Understanding Children will provide you with the opportunity to begin thinking about how you study. Some areas of studying you may find easy, others more of a challenge. For most people studying effectively takes time and practice but hopefully it will become something that you enjoy.

So far you have been briefly introduced to each of the six areas of study which will be covered in *Understanding Children*. This is your first opportunity to reflect upon how confident you feel in these areas by completing the following.

1   Look back through the course book and write down the six *effective study* areas.

2   Write down four different sources of evidence.

3   What do you understand by the word 'argument' in the context of studying?

4   List at least two examples of parallel time that you have been able to use.

5   Write down two things that you like about how you write and two things that you would like to change.

APPENDIX TO UNIT 1

Effective study   Essay writing

The following activity will take you through from your first experiences of language to the present. You are asked to think about the questions posed and respond by writing in the boxes. There are four sets of questions and each set should take you about five minutes to do. Your notes can form the basis of a discussion with your tutor.

ACTIVITY A	LANGUAGE HISTORY

Allow about 20 minutes

The language you use, both spoken and written language, reflects the person you are. Where you were born and grew up plays an important part in determining the language you speak. The language(s) that your parents and family spoke was (were) probably the most important influence when you were small, and then your friends, schooling and jobs all added to the pool of language from which you chose.

Reflecting on your personal language background can help you to understand how your use of language developed. This is true whether English is your first, second or even third language.

At the end of the exercise you can read the responses of some other students who have completed this activity.

Table 6 Your language history

From birth to school age

Which language(s) or dialect(s) did you hear first, do you think? From whom?

Which one did you learn to speak first?

How many language(s) or dialect(s) were you using by the time you went to school?

With whom did you use them?

I was born in 1939, Palestine
Arabic

My parents and siblings
Arabic

one

Family

Through school

Think about the place(s) where you went to school. Where did you go to nursery or kindergarten; first/primary/middle school; secondary school?

Which language did you learn to read and write in? Did this differ from your pre-school language experience?

Which language or dialect did the teachers or instructors use? Did this affect your own use of language? Why?

Primary School
Kufer Yasref
Palestine

Arabic
NO

Work and study since school

How have the jobs you have done, since school, affected your language use?

Think about speaking, listening, reading and writing. Do you still use all the languages and dialects you have learned?

In your experience of study since school, what more have you learned about your own use of language?

I have learned English as a Second language
NO
I like language. I think I could have a flair for it

COMMENT

Here are some extracts from the language histories of others that you might like to compare with your own.

Table 7 Extracts from others' language histories

From birth to school age

Which language(s) or dialect(s) did you hear first, do you think? From whom?

Which one did you learn to speak first?

How many language(s) or dialect(s) were you using by the time you went to school?

With whom did you use them?

Extract A

I was born in Birmingham in the Midlands in 1950, the last of five children. English was the first language I heard and spoke although for some reason I did not utter a word till I was three years of age. My parents always encouraged me to speak 'properly' which meant sounding Ts, not swearing, not speaking in a 'Brummie' accent.

Extract B

The first language I spoke was English for as long as I can remember. Around our household my father tried and succeeded to speak the 'Queen's English', whereas my mother spoke Jamaican Creole. I found the tone and contents of our oral communication warm, friendly, homely and very funny at times, because of things my mother would say.

Through school

Think about the place(s) where you went to school. Where did you go to nursery or kindergarten; first/ primary/middle school; secondary school?

Which language did you learn to read and write in? Did this differ from your pre-school language experience?

Which language or dialect did the teachers or instructors use? Did this affect your own use of language? Why?

Extract C

I was educated at a convent school in North-East Brazil until I was fifteen years old (1950s and early 1960s). The nuns were Brazilian and German (refugees from the Nazis). I grew up hearing German, although I couldn't speak it. I started learning French at school when I was ten and English when I was eleven. My mother was very keen on education, and we children had private tuition in these languages, from native speakers. My private English tutor was actually Welsh.

Extract D

My first language is German and I started learning English at school at the age of eleven. I continued until I stopped studying at 20. Some teachers had been to America and so their teaching was often American English.

Work and study since school

How have the jobs you have done, since school, affected your language use?

Think about speaking, listening, reading and writing. Do you still use all the languages and dialects you have learned?

In your experience of study since school, what more have you learned about your own use of language?

Extract E

After leaving school I trained as a nursery nurse and here I learned a completely different language; for example, 'developmental milestones', 'lack of stimulation', 'environmental influences', 'temper tantrums'. This is what I would term professional language or jargon. In addition, I learned that, although people used English, the meaning attached to the same word could vary greatly, for example 'to beat a child' to an English person means beating with a strap or similar object, but to a Caribbean person this means a smack. The realization came from working and mixing socially with people from the Caribbean. I found the Caribbean use of English to be warm and friendly yet at times harsh as well as very descriptive, creating a picture of what was being expressed very quickly.

Extract F

Just before leaving secondary school, most of the school-leavers were applying for jobs (there were plenty to go round in those days) and I remember one particular incident. A girl from another class had applied for a shop assistant's job at John Lewis's department store in Oxford Street, and she was turned down because of her accent. That was the first time I was aware of the connection between class, accent and prejudice. I was working class and expected to fit into the niche provided. The aspirations for my contemporaries and I were to get a trade and that's what most of us did.

Thinking about your own answers and the extracts from other students' language histories, you will see that there is a great variety among us. Variation in spoken English comes from dialect and from accent, which vary according to where we were born, where we live or which social group we come from. Accent and dialect are a very important part of who we are, and many of us will hang on to them in certain circumstances, such as with family and friends, but adopt a different style of language in more formal situations and in academic writing. This switching between varieties of language is useful, but we need to know which 'voice' is appropriate for different situations.

Finally, we'd like you to focus on your Open University studies and consider the following questions.

- How will your experience help you be an effective student? For example, you might understand more about the nature of language itself, or know that some languages are seen as being of a higher status than others.
- Which language skills do you think you need to develop now, if you are to become an even better student?
- Are there any specific skills you will need for your particular course? You may find useful advice on this in your Assignment Booklet.

If you prefer you could try this activity online: http://www3.open.ac.uk/learners-guide/learning-skills/english/

(Adapted from *The Effective Use of English: Online Student Toolkit*, Open University 2001)

Effective study Reading for study

The following activity is intended to help you think about your experiences of reading. We have provided a table which contains some questions for you to think about. Jodie has also completed this activity, reflecting on her early reading experiences.

ACTIVITY B   READING HISTORY

Allow about 10 minutes

Read through Jodie's answers and then spend 5 minutes thinking about your own memories and feelings about writing, before putting your ideas down on the blank table. The notes are only to help you get your ideas in order, but you should then use them as the basis of a discussion with your tutor on the phone.

Table 8 Jodie's thoughts on reading

How and where did you first learn to read? Do you have memories of how you felt about it?	I didn't learn to read until I went to school – story telling was important but we didn't have many books in the house. I was very excited about learning to read, but it took a while to 'click'. I was great at working out the story from the pictures, but when we had to learn from flash cards I was lost!
Do you have any memories of reading at school? Was it enjoyable or did you worry or feel bored?	My main memory is of the book being so boring. I guess looking back the simple books didn't use enough vocabulary to make them interesting, but I was used to such wonderful stories I couldn't see the point. It was only when we got on to more interesting stories that I really took off with my reading, but I still tend to read 'word by word' which feels painfully slow to me. If I don't, I feel as if I am cheating!

Do you feel that you had any particular challenges to overcome in learning to read – such as speaking a first language or dialect other than English, or being dyslexic?	I can't say I had any particular problems. I did speak with a local accent – not really a full Scouse though – which sometimes caused problems when recognizing words we were supposed to work out from the phonetic alphabet. But then so many words aren't spelt how you think they should be anyway!
Do you have any anxieties, hopes or expectations about reading for higher education study?	Yes! I am mostly worried that I read too slowly and won't understand the words used – not normal words but highfaluting type ones. I am worried I'll fall behind and look silly if my tutor thinks I haven't understood the reading properly when I do my assignments. I don't really think I am university material to be honest, but I am interested in the subjects.
Do you feel that the way in which you read is still influenced by any of your early reading experiences such as the way in which you were taught?	Maybe – in that I read word by word, and that I get bored easily! And I suppose I don't think of reading as being fun or really 'me' in the way talking about stuff is.
Do you think that you may find some additional support with improving reading techniques helpful?	I'll let you know!
Anything else?	

Table 9   Your thoughts on reading

How and where did you first learn to read? Do you have memories of how you felt about it?	I have very vague memories about learning to read. I am now 68 years old.
Do you have any memories of reading at school? Was it enjoyable or did you worry or feel bored?	I can remember when I first read a novel. I will have been about 14 years old. I had great pleasure reading. I can still remember the name of a character was Madge.

Do you feel that you had any particular challenges to overcome in learning to read – such as speaking a first language or dialect other than English, or being dyslexic?	I am self thought in English. It was very Challenging. At the age of 46 I went to College and did O Level in English and O Level in Sociology.
Do you have any anxieties, hopes or expectations about reading for higher education study?	Not really.
Do you feel that the way in which you read is still influenced by any of your early reading experiences such as the way in which you were taught?	No. I love reading but I would like to read faster.
Do you think that you may find some additional support with improving reading techniques helpful?	I hope so.
Anything else?	I am curias as to what I will accomplish by the end of the course.

COMMENT

We hope that completing this exercise will open up a discussion as well as enable you to spend some time thinking about your experiences of reading. There are many factors which influence the way in which people read, and there is no 'right' way to do it. If you do have any unpleasant memories of reading in school or since, hopefully reading *Understanding Children* will give you some different and more positive experiences. You will return to thinking about reading later in the course, but if you feel that this is an area that you would like to focus on you could look at the Student Toolkit on *Reading and Note Taking*. You can either ask your tutor how to get a copy or if you are online you can look at it on the web:

http://www3.open.ac.uk/learners-guide/learning-skills/
additional_resources/taking_notes.htm

Look this up on line

2 CHILDREN HAVING A SAY

1 NEGOTIATIONS AT HOME

CORE QUESTIONS

- How can parents involve children in resolving family difficulties with young children?
- Why is it important to think about the everyday experiences of young children when trying to resolve family problems?
- How can adults listen more effectively to young children?

Figure 19 Ryan

RYAN

First term at Infant School & Bedtime problems

The Family have learned a lot about Mia's abilities and her view of the world. Daisy and Ryan still occasionally find their little sister an intrusion into their activities and interests, but they also love showing off to their friends about all the amazing things that she can do and how she communicates.

Jodie has also been reflecting on they way in which Ryan has grown from the baby he still seemed to be 18 months ago to the little boy he is at four and a half. Ryan moved from his nursery school, which he attended half-time, to the reception class at Daisy's infant and junior school three months ago. Eamon and Jodie have found the move from shared care at home through to a half-time nursery and now to a full school day, although emotional, a fairly smooth transition. Reflecting with Eamon on his first term, Jodie wonders how Ryan has experienced it. He seems happy and settled at school, although the worries about what he eats have arisen again, and there have been increasing problems around bedtimes recently. Ryan's teacher has reassured her that many children become unsettled for a period after starting school, but Jodie is still worried.

The Problem !!

Different Approaches to managing family Conflicts with young Children !

1.1 BEDTIMES

In this section the Family are challenged by finding a resolution to unhappy bedtimes for Ryan. In the Family's search for a resolution they encounter and reflect upon a number of different approaches to managing conflict with young children. These approaches are not specific to bedtimes. They are all used to varying degrees with young children, but conflict over bedtimes is a common experience and is used here to illustrate a spectrum of approaches.

UNHAPPY BEDTIMES

Conflict at B/T.

Ryan is allowed to go to bed latter at his Dad's house, than his Mum's,

Ryan:

> I hate bedtimes. I can't sleep and Mum and Eamon won't let me keep the light on. I never go to bed this early at Dad's. Why can't I go to bed at the same time as Daisy and Mia? It's not fair! I can hear everybody else downstairs and I'm stuck up here on my own. I wish I could sleep with Mum like Mia does.

Jodie and Eamon have been worried about the difficulties which they all have in persuading Ryan to go to bed at his usual time. Ryan has always been a child who sleeps well and until recently there have not been any problems around bedtimes. Increasingly, however, Ryan refuses to get ready for bed without Jodie or Eamon getting cross. When he is finally in bed, he comes back downstairs three or four times a night saying that he can't sleep or asking for food or drinks. It is not unusual now for Ryan to be still awake when Jodie and Eamon finally put Mia down after her last feed. Mia often has a nap in the afternoon, and is therefore awake until around midnight when Jodie, who has continued to give Mia one breastfeed before she goes to sleep, and Eamon finally go to bed. Consequently Ryan is overtired in the morning and grumpy when they get him up and ready for school.

Figure 20 Ryan in bed

A common problem?

The problem faced by the Family is a common and often distressing challenge of parenting. Bedtimes can be a real struggle for many parents and children from babies right up to young people. The importance of a regular bedtime will vary from family to family. In some families the belief that children should go to bed earlier than adults or at specific age-related times will seem odd. The assumption that children should have different bedtimes from adults is based upon a particular view of childhood as a period of time when people under a certain age need to be treated differently from adults.

The belief that 'childhood' should be preserved as a time for play and learning is not universal. For example in societies where families' main concern is survival due to poverty and scarce natural resources, 'children' are expected to work alongside adults by necessity, although education and play in many forms are also part of their lives. What is common, however, for most children is that 'bedtime' will depend on factors such as the specific requirements of the next day, the age of the child and the individual family circumstances and customs.

PROBLEMS FOR THE FAMILY?

Ryan's reluctance to keep to a specified bedtime is causing problems. Ryan has to get up in time for school in the mornings and if he goes to sleep late he will either be late for school or overtired. This is a cause of concern for Jodie who is worried about Ryan making a good start at his new school. Eamon, who is responsible for taking Ryan to school, is worried about getting into regular 'nagging' battles in the morning in order to avoid them both being late for school or work. Daisy is becoming increasingly resentful of Ryan getting away with staying up later than she does. Jodie and Eamon also feel the need to have some quiet time for themselves and Mia at the end of the day. Ryan's 'behaviour' has become a problem for the whole family.

The problem gets out of control!!

Eamon and Jodie decide that they need to do something. They don't feel able to change Ryan's behaviour. Jodie has even resorted to threatening to smack Ryan, and both Jodie and Eamon have lost their tempers and shouted at him. It feels to them as if things are getting out of control. They need to resolve the bedtime problem. But how?

ACTIVITY 15   MANAGING BEDTIMES

Allow 10 minutes

You may have experienced difficult bedtimes as a parent or as a child. Your experiences, just as anyone else's, will have been influenced by the expectations and circumstances of your family. This diversity of experiences means that there can be many different causes and responses to unhappy bedtimes. Spend 10 minutes thinking about as many ways as you can to respond to Ryan's difficulties.

COMMENT

Did you think of a few strategies? There are lots of different ways in which parents and carers manage this problem, and there is no 'secret answer' to resolving it for all families. As you read through this section you may come across some of the strategies you have thought of in this activity and will be given the opportunity to think about the advantages and disadvantages as well as ideas for putting them into practice. You may find that you disagree with some of the discussion in this section. Parenting is both very personal and in some ways private to families – but increasingly it is also a public concern. By this we mean that governments and international bodies increasingly regulate the way in which both paid carers and parents care for children. The views which you will come across in *Understanding Children* broadly represent those of researchers and people working with children and their families.

TALKING TO RYAN

Jodie and Eamon begin by trying to talk to Ryan. Unfortunately this conversation does not go well. Jodie asks Ryan to join Eamon and herself to talk at the kitchen table. Ryan reluctantly sits down, but faces the TV in the next room, swinging his legs and humming the cartoon theme tune to himself. Jodie and Eamon become frustrated, and ask him why he doesn't want to talk with them. '*It's boring*'. When Jodie asks Ryan how he is feeling he says '*Happy, happy, happy!*' and asks if he can go back to the TV room. In exasperation Jodie and Eamon give up. It doesn't seem as if talking to Ryan is going to help.

Together they decide to make a list of all the possible sources of ideas and advice they could go to for suggestions. Here is their list:

> The internet
>
> Mrs Dee (Ryan's class teacher)
>
> Rosalind

Is 'Ryan's behaviour' the problem?

The Family is not unusual in their initial response to Ryan's resistance to going to bed. When a child acts in a way which does not conform, they may be seen by adults as being the cause of the problem and in need of discipline or correction.

LOOKING ON THE INTERNET

So far Jodie and Eamon have tried to make Ryan keep to the family expectations of him by reminding him of the rules repeatedly. When this has failed they have threatened smacking and lost their tempers to the point of shouting at Ryan. Jodie in particular is concerned about her own reactions to Ryan's behaviour and is worried about losing control herself. Her first avenue for advice is the internet. She feels embarrassed to talk to anyone outside of the immediate family about her concerns.

Effective study   Reflection

Studying involves seeking information from different sources. Whether your information comes in the form of written text, audio/video recordings or a web page, it represents the views or opinions of the 'author' or editor. It is important to look for information on a subject from different sources so that you find as many different points of view as possible. In much the same way as you will select evidence and build an argument in your essays, these sources will reflect the points of view of the authors. When you have lots of different views on a subject, you can then start really thinking about what you think by 'weighing up the evidence', deciding who has the most convincing view. It is important when you are studying, therefore, to reflect upon not only what you read, view or listen to but also upon whose opinions are represented and whether they are balanced or biased (one sided).

Understanding Children provides you with all of the sources that you need, but you will notice that we have not written all of the book ourselves. We have also included ideas from other people, some of whom we will agree with more than others! These ideas appear in the form of extracts from books or articles, and audio and video recordings. We have also included some pages from the internet. Using the internet for study does require some caution. This is because no one has necessarily checked that what is written there is true or based on research. The pages we have used have been put on the internet by nationally respected organizations with a good reputation for research. This does not mean, however, that they do not have a particular view or perspective which they want to get across to readers.

In the next activity you will read an extract from a website produced by the NSPCC.

ACTIVITY 16	IS SMACKING OK?

Allow about 20 minutes

Before you begin reading the extract that Jodie found, jot down your thoughts on the following questions:

- What would you expect the NSPCC's view to be on smacking and why?
- Would you trust information given to you by the NSPCC? Why?
- Can you think of an organization or an example of a person who might have very different views?

Keep your notes, and now have a look at the following extract which Jodie found. As you read, check whether your 'guess' about the position of the NSPCC was correct and suggest some reasons why you either agree or disagree with this extract.

Encouraging better behaviour

Many parents say their children are the most important part of their lives. They bring joy and laughter and give you a stake in the future. But being a parent isn't always easy. It can be challenging and exhausting. At such times parents who are normally loving and caring can find themselves 'losing it' and hitting their children.

Most parents don't think hitting children is right, yet in times of stress, anger or frustration find themselves lashing out. But many feel guilty afterwards and want to find better ways of handling difficult behaviour.

Positive parenting and positive discipline
Saying sorry

Working at positive discipline takes a lot of energy. No parent can do it perfectly all the time. All parents have behaved in ways they regret – shouting or smacking. If it happens, say you are sorry, make up and try again. This teaches children a valuable lesson.

Why smacking is never a good idea

Parents may believe there are occasions when only a smack will do. For example, your child is really cheeky and disobedient; your toddler runs into the road; one of your children bites a playmate. It can be tempting to think a smack sorts out these incidents quickly, but it does nothing to teach your child how you want him to behave. Instead:

- It gives a bad example of how to handle strong emotions.
- It may lead children to hit or bully others.
- They may lie, or hide feelings to avoid smacking.
- It can make defiant, uncooperative behaviour worse, so discipline gets even harder.
- Children feel resentful and angry, which can spoil family relationships if it goes on for a long time.

I was smacked as a child – did my parents get it wrong?

These days we know a great deal more about why children behave as they do, and about the effects of smacking. Our parents did the best they could at the time. Modern parents choose parenting without the pain, for child or adults.

Top ten ways to be a great parent without smacking

- Give love and warmth as much as possible.
- Have clear simple rules and limits.
- Be a good example.
- Praise good behaviour so it will increase.
- Ignore behaviour you don't want repeated.
- Criticise behaviours, not your child.
- Reward good behaviour by hugs and kisses.
- Distract younger children or use humour.
- Allow children some control – choices, joint decisions.
- If a punishment is necessary, then removal of privileges, 'time out', or natural consequences all work better than smacking.

(Adapted from: NSPCC, 2002, *Encouraging better behaviour* (online), http://www.nspcc.org.uk/html/Home/Needadvice/ encouragingbetterbehaviour.htm)

Yes I believe smacking is wrong. and a parent should appologise for smacking a child.

COMMENT

How did you get on? Were you surprised that the NSPCC suggest that smacking should not be used to chastise children, and that if it is used parents should apologise to their children?

As NSPCC is a national organization set up to combat child cruelty, you may not have been surprised that they took a firm stand against smacking. Would you be convinced by their position, though?

This extract does not attempt to explain why the NSPCC believe that smacking is harmful (although they do elsewhere) so they depend upon their reputation to convince you. The NSPCC is a well-established national organization and does speak with the authority of being the only voluntary organization with the power, alongside Social Services, to carry out investigations into child abuse.

An individual with no expertise in the subject or a smaller organization might have less influence. I expect that you know people, as we do, who either firmly believe in the benefits of smacking or, more commonly, believe that it causes no particular harm. You may believe this yourself. But if an individual wrote a website giving these views, without the support of research, their opinions would not be very reliable as evidence for your essays. *NO*

Resource Booklet? where?

If you have access to the internet and want to search for more information, you could start with these kinds of national organizations or government sites. We have given you some links in the further reading section in the Resource Booklet.

Smacking is a very emotive subject and many parents have strong feelings about whether it is right or wrong. In some countries, such as Sweden, smacking children is against the law and the governments in England and Scotland have also been debating whether to make smacking illegal. Despite many European countries outlawing smacking by parents, in England parents are not prevented from using smacking as a punishment for their own children. The NSPCC, along with other organizations concerned with children's rights, take the position that at best smacking is not an effective way to manage difficult behaviour. The contradictory legal position on smacking provides a very confusing message for parents and children.

Anti-smacking messages from childcare organizations do not suggest that parents should not attempt to guide and control their children's behaviour. The final point on the NSPCC list suggests the use of rewards and 'time out' as an alternative and more effective way to manage children's behaviour.

Jodie finds the NSPCC advice reassuring – neither Jodie nor Eamon favour smacking and the site offers some interesting advice about alternative strategies as well as telling them that they are not alone in their fear of losing control and smacking Ryan.

The idea of using a star chart appeals to Eamon and Jodie, and they contact Mrs Dee, Ryan's school teacher, to ask for some advice about managing behaviour using rewards. Mrs Dee suggests that the couple read the following extract which she had found on an internet site.

Sleep: star charts approach

Star charts can be very helpful with the older child (3.5 years+) who is having problems with sleeping. The idea behind the use of star charts is that the child gets rewarded for the behaviour the parents are looking for. The focus of the charts is positive and this approach does not involve any form of punishment. These charts can be great and catch the child's imagination.

They work best in the initial period and therefore when deciding to use them the parents need to be clear on what exact behaviour they are looking for. All that is needed to make a star chart is a sheet of paper and some colouring pencils or sticky stars, circles etc. The page is divided into days and if the child achieves the task set they receive a star or a circle that day. Or indeed they could colour in that day the colour of their choice.

Another chart that could be used for this purpose would be a sticker poster. Your child can put the stickers on as they achieve the goal set for them. If your child does not achieve the task then nothing is said and that day's space on the page remains blank. When your child has three (can be variable) stars, circles, coloured days, they receive a treat that has already been agreed. It is best when deciding on the treat that it is something small and easy to arrange. It does not have to be sweets or toys – it could be a game of football with Dad, a chance to do some cooking/ baking, whatever it is your child is into. These charts work through the mixture of the praise your child receives when they manage to get a star etc. and the sense of achievement they experience on reaching their goal.

(RollerCoaster.ie, 2003, *Sleep: star charts approach* (online), http://www.rollercoaster.ie/sleep/star_charts.asp)

Eamon and Jodie have always been sceptical about reward systems, but decided that a star chart might be worth a go with Ryan if it just focused on bedtimes. Jodie and Eamon asked Ryan what he thought would be a fair reward if he settled in bed quietly within 15 minutes of being asked. Ryan chose some bright stickers of animals to stick on a chart; he could then choose which one to put on the chart each morning after he had gone to bed on time. Jodie and Eamon also told Ryan that once he had three stickers in a row, they would give him a treat which he could choose. Ryan was very excited about the star chart and seemed motivated.

Monday	Tuesday	Wednesday	Thursday	Friday	Saturday	Sunday
🐑		🐖		🐬	🐰	
	🐎		🐰			
🐖		🐑	🐬	🐎		

Figure 21 A star chart

After four weeks, however, Eamon and Jodie were questioning how useful it was. A number of problems had arisen. First they found it very difficult to enforce the chart – Ryan often took a long time getting into his bed and settling down, as usual, and then wanted to know if he had earned his sticker. If he was told that he had not, Ryan became distressed or angry and was even less likely to settle. He did have several really good nights, and won his chosen trip to a safari park the second week. The following two weeks he only won two stickers, and Jodie and Eamon felt they could not increase the target to four stickers in a week. Eventually Ryan became bored and disappointed that he was not winning more treats. Bedtimes had improved for a week or so, but then things gradually returned to the way they had been and Jodie began to wonder if Ryan's star chart was really making any difference. Eamon and Jodie decided to talk to Rosalind about their concerns.

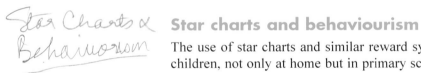

Star charts and behaviourism

The use of star charts and similar reward systems is common with young children, not only at home but in primary schools and also by social workers with children who have particular emotional or behavioural needs. The theory behind such methods stem from a branch of psychology called *behaviourism*. Over at least the past 30 years behaviourism has had many forms, but in simple terms it is based upon the idea that children's (and adults') behaviour can be changed through learning and association. If a child associates certain behaviour with bad outcomes they will avoid it. If they associate it with good outcomes, they will repeat it. 'Punishments' might include having parental attention temporarily withdrawn or being excluded from group activities for a short while, sometimes referred to as 'time out'. Rewards are focused on more than 'punishments', particularly with younger children, and rewards are used to encourage desired behaviour and discourage undesirable behaviour.

There has been increasing criticism of behavioural strategies with children, primarily on the basis that, if they work at all, the benefits or changes in behaviour are short-lived. Criticism has also been made due to the fact that often one person, the adult, is manipulating or coercing the behaviour of another, the child. This issue will be explored further below. However, where

For Ersay.

the child is involved in discussions about behaviour, this interaction between parent and child may in itself eventually bring about a positive change. A reduction in family tension can result where parents' focus is redirected towards encouraging positive achievements rather than getting cross.

THE WIDER FAMILY

Rosalind:

> You need to listen to the child. He has a lot to cope with! And it is no good just getting on at him when he is naughty. Try to ignore him – he will only do it more just to get your attention away from the baby. Spend some time with him on his own, Jodie – he loves that and you will get a break from Mia. I will have her for you, and Daisy too. Have some time on your own together. Have some fun, give him some love and don't be so wound up and worried. He is a child – he will settle down.

Jodie is slightly reassured by Rosalind but still feels that she needs help understanding Ryan's feelings. She returns to the NSPCC site and notices a link from this to another interesting site which makes reference to new babies in stepfamilies. Jodie reads the advice on this site, but she also decides to set up a discussion with Eamon, Graham and herself about their concerns regarding Ryan. Graham has been having Ryan to stay overnight a little more often recently, to help Jodie out when she is at home with the children alone because Eamon is on a night shift. Jodie has been grateful for this and is hesitant to question Graham's parenting as a result. As soon as the topic is raised, however, it is clear that Graham is 'making the most' of his time with Ryan by letting him stay up very late, watching films and playing. Graham is quite happy to allow Ryan to stay up until he falls asleep on the sofa, and then put him to bed.

ACTIVITY 17   STEPFAMILIES

Allow about 15 minutes

Read through the following short extracts from web pages published by Parentline Plus. Thinking about Ryan's situation, underline any points which you think might apply to him.

A new baby in a stepfamily

This situation can cause additional stresses and strains because it affects a number of different people and relationships, which may already be fragile. Existing children may feel that their father or mother won't love them anymore and that the new baby will take their place.

All children may feel this at the birth of a younger sibling but it can be harder for children where the new baby is part of their parent's new life with a new partner. Sometimes they can feel second best; for other children their new half brother/sister may help them to get more involved with their stepfamily.

Managing family changes

All families have their ups and downs. Many of the complications happen because life throws many challenges and changes at us, and we all react differently to these.

Key life changes bring confusion into the most well ordered lives. Birth, death, marriage, changing schools, changing jobs, moving house, leaving home, divorce, remarriage ... all these events can leave us questioning fundamental beliefs and values.

All change is difficult – it involves losses as well as gains. Often, we believe we are meant to be happy and excited about the change, and this leaves very little space to feel sad about the things and people we may leave behind.

Allow yourself and others in the family to have mixed feelings about any changes. Different members of your family may feel differently about the same event. Try to let everyone express how they feel. Feelings do change over time, and we do all get used to changes.

(Parentline Plus, no date, *Parents: get information about ... New baby* and *Managing family changes* (online), http://www.parentlineplus.org.uk/data/parents)

COMMENT

If you have experienced living as part of a stepfamily, or a 'reconstituted family', then this activity may have raised some strong feelings for you. Such families can face even harder challenges than first relationships and the arrival of a new baby can be particularly difficult as well as joyful. The points we underlined included:

- Ryan is feeling both excited and involved in the arrival of Mia.
- He may also be feeling a little pushed out, or in second or even third place.
- He has also recently moved to a new school and may have both excited, happy feelings and sad ones that he finds hard to express

Are star charts and 'time out' the end of the story?

While parents and professionals sometimes find strategies such as reward charts and 'time out' effective in managing some behaviour with some children, the benefits are generally limited and short-lived.

The above list suggests that the root causes of children's (and adults') behaviour is often complex and multifaceted. Ryan may not know himself why he is finding bedtimes difficult, hence his reluctance to talk about the problem with his mum and Eamon. Listening to children and helping them both understand and talk about their feelings is a vital part of parenting and is a skill which many adults need to learn or relearn.

1.2 HELPING CHILDREN TALK ABOUT FEELINGS

PUTTING IDEAS TOGETHER

Jodie and Eamon have learned a lot over the past few weeks through their research and reflection on Ryan's recent experiences. Rosalind's words had a particular impact, as did a quote which Jodie read in a book which discussed alternatives to using rewards and punishments with children.

Effective study   Developing and demonstrating understanding

When you are studying in higher education you will find that it is not only important to learn about new ideas and facts; you will also be expected to develop and demonstrate your understanding. One way of doing this is through the way in which you organize ideas and facts. This involves selecting specific points from your course and using them to explain or argue a point of view to your reader. This process of organizing information is where your own creativity and individuality comes into study – you begin to have an input as well as the authors and tutors of the course.

People vary in the way in which they find it helpful to organize their thinking. Some people find it easier to think in pictures or diagrams; some people prefer to write things out, maybe in a logical order. For those who like pictures and diagrams, using a mind map can be a really good way to organize ideas and information. There are no strict rules about what a mind

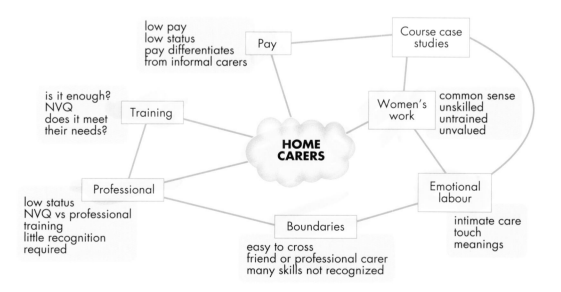

Figure 22 Example of a mind map

Question

map should look like, but the idea is that you put your question or main idea in the middle and then draw connections to other ideas or information which you think is relevant. Figure 22 shows an example of a mind map completed for a different course about home carers. Home carers provide care in the homes of people who are disabled, elderly or unwell and this mind map illustrates some of the contradictions in their role. Their work is often undervalued (low pay, little training and status) but is often complex and demanding.

| ACTIVITY 18 | BEING A DETECTIVE |

Allow about 20 minutes

In this activity you will have the opportunity to try using a mind map. First re-read the account of Jodie's first attempt to talk to Ryan (which is reprinted for you here) and then read the quotation from Alfie Kohn which set Jodie thinking.

> Jodie and Eamon begin by trying to talk to Ryan. Unfortunately this conversation does not go well. Jodie asks Ryan to join Eamon and herself to talk at the kitchen table. Ryan reluctantly sits down, but faces the TV in the next room, swinging his legs and humming the cartoon theme tune to himself. Jodie and Eamon become frustrated, and ask him why he doesn't want to talk with them. *'It's boring'*. When Jodie asks Ryan how he is feeling he says *'Happy, happy, happy!'* and asks if he can go back to the TV room. In exasperation Jodie and Eamon give up. It doesn't seem as if talking to Ryan is go to help.

Younger children cannot always identify and verbalize their motives. Five-year-olds do not pause reflectively and say, 'Well, Daddy, I guess I slugged Zachary because I'm displacing my emotional turmoil caused by hearing you and Mommy yell at each other so much'. They are more likely to shrug and mutter, 'I dunno'… **When the child cannot be forthcoming, parents and teachers have to become detectives, looking for clues as to possible causes and trying out hypotheses tentatively in the process of working out a solution**.

(Kohn, 1993, pp. 237–8; bold added)

Now, focus on the **bold** words in the reading above. Using all of the information you have about Ryan and his family, together with anything you have learned in this section and your own experiences, try acting 'detective' and draw a mind map that includes information, ideas and hypotheses which might help you understand the reasons for Ryan's unhappiness at bedtimes. To get you started, you could put 'Unhappy bedtimes' in the middle.

COMMENT

How did you get on? Figure 23 shows my mind map. Don't worry if yours looks very different; mind maps should be individual and creative. What is more, only you need to understand them as they are to help your own thinking!

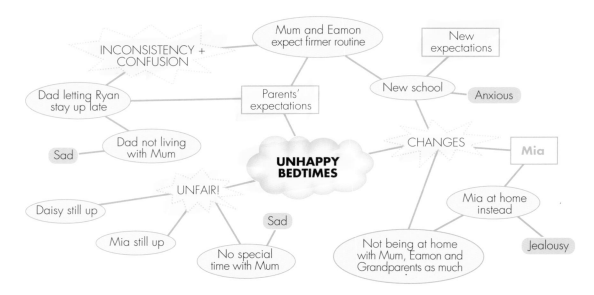

Figure 23 Unhappy bedtimes mind map

For those of you who don't find pictures and diagrams helpful, here is another way of organizing the same information:

Unhappy bedtimes

- New expectations of school resulting from the move from full-time care at home and with his grandparents represented change from a familiar routines.
- The arrival of a new baby. This baby could be a source of jealousy for Ryan in particular because Mia takes his place as the youngest in the family and is also the only natural child of both Jodie and Eamon.
- Expectations of Ryan's routines have been strengthened from Jodie and Eamon since he started school.
- This expectation has not been matched by Graham, who is letting Ryan stay up very late. This could give Ryan a very confusing message about why he has to go to bed.
- Ryan beginning school has come at the same time as Jodie and Eamon are staying up caring for Mia. From Ryan's perspective his place as the baby of the family has gone and he needs to find a new role in the family.
- Starting a new school means being away from home more, leaving Mia with parental figures who had been devoting their time to him.
- Although Ryan's memory of living with Graham is probably limited, he may be aware of an uncertainly around the predictability of his relationship with his father and may feel more anxious about this since the birth of Eamon's own daughter.

Many children of Ryan's age have little experience of talking about or even recognizing their own feelings. Professionals working with children have increasingly identified the importance of helping them to recognize and name their feelings. Games that encourage children to name the expressions on faces are commonly used in nursery and reception classes, and versions are even available in toyshops.

Lonely/sad

A

Figure 24
Teddy Faces game

Toys, pictures and the arts (visual and performing) are used to help children express their feelings because play is a more familiar way of communicating than talking, particularly for young children. Setting up a 'child-friendly' context for listening to children is very important. It requires adults to help children feel as comfortable as possible. This will involve thinking about both the 'place' and the 'pace' of interactions with children in order to help them express themselves. The 'place' needs to be somewhere familiar and relaxed for a child where they can be engaged in play and sit comfortably, ideally on the floor or child-sized chairs. It is also important that the 'pace', or speed, is set by the child. Pushing a child for quick results may not only put the child under pressure so that they do not want to interact at all, but may also be placing unrealistic expectations on them – maybe they do not understand their feelings or have the words to express them, or maybe they do not want to express them at all.

ACTIVITY 19	LISTENING TO RYAN

Allow about 15 minutes

Alfie Kohn (1993) suggests that you may need to be a detective, guessing at the underlying causes of children's concerns, but there are also some other ways in which you can communicate with children in a way which helps them feel more at ease. Think about the way in which Jodie and Eamon set up their conversation with Ryan and try to think of ways that might suggest a more 'child-centred' approach. What could Jodie and Eamon do to help Ryan share his thoughts about why bedtimes have become difficult? It might help

Child centred approach

you to try to imagine that you are a five year old or think about a five year old you know. Try to write down at least three ideas that you could try to help Ryan express his feelings.

How did you get on? There is no one answer to this question, and much will depend upon Ryan as an individual child. Here are just a few ideas:

- Sitting at the kitchen table may have seemed comfortable and informal for Jodie and Eamon – but would this have been Ryan's choice? He may have preferred to be sprawled on the floor or on beanbags with his toys.
- Spend some time with Ryan doing something he really enjoys, such as playing with his trains, or any activity which he chooses.
- Join in with the game and remember that for children play is an important way of communicating.
- Allow Ryan to lead the 'conversation' as much as possible; as an adult it is important that you are interested in his agenda, rather than imposing one of your own.
- Be honest with him. Tell Ryan that you are worried about him and need his help to understand.
- Use any knowledge you do have about Ryan to guess at what may be worrying him, or making him feel bad. Don't worry about getting it wrong – Ryan will tell you or ignore you. If you do guess right you may open up the door for him to tell you more.
- Just repeating back to children what they have said to you, maybe in slightly different words, shows them that you are listening and understanding them – 'attending' to them or being attentive.
- Ryan may be reluctant to tell you his feelings and thoughts in case you get cross. Give him lots of praise and encouragement. If you feel yourself getting cross or frustrated, Ryan will probably pick this up so it might be better to stop and try again later when you are more relaxed.

Did Jodie and Eamon go wrong?

As adults, Jodie and Eamon sat down with an intention to talk about the 'problem'. They were setting the agenda. Ryan's response to this may have been that he was being 'told off' and that he was not going to be listened to. 'It's boring' could be interpreted as 'This isn't relevant for me – you're not going to listen to what I have to say'. Jodie and Eamon were working at an adult's pace; they had been thinking about the problem for a while but Ryan had not had time to think or find his words. He may not know why he feels bad or why he is finding it difficult to sleep – he may believe that he is just being 'naughty' and may have no idea how he can get himself out of a cycle of feeling bad and getting into trouble. With a discussion set up in such a way as to convince Ryan that he was not going to be listened to, his aim was to say the right thing and escape from the room. If he declared himself fine and happy and promised to be good, then he could probably get back to the TV! Where children genuinely are not clear about *why* they are feeling bad, they will need help from thoughtful adults (or other children) to help them work out what is going on for them.

1.3 POWER AND PARENTING

Jodie and Eamon have probably not consciously considered themselves as 'powerful' during their exploration of strategies to respond to Ryan's difficulties. In fact they may well at times have felt at a loss and that Ryan was the person in the driving seat. Ultimately, however, adults are more powerful than children; they are usually physically stronger, they hold and control the family resources and they also have emotional power over their children. Children are dependent physically and emotionally on adults.

Alfie Kohn, whose writing Jodie came across, provides a three-step model for solving problems between parents and children. He starts from the basic idea that in most adult–child encounters the primary objective of the adult is to 'make' the child obey; the second question is: 'how can I make them obey?' So, for Jodie and Eamon: 'Ryan is not going to bed at his bedtime; how can we make him do so?' Alfie Kohn asks his reader to move back a step and consider the following.

Alfie Kohn's three Cs

Kohn defines the three Cs as:

> Content
>
> Collaboration
>
> Choice.

He suggests that, when a problem arises, the adult should first consider the **content** of their request or expectation of the child. Is the expectation reasonable? This involves looking at the request from the child's perspective. Is the child capable of complying? Does the child have a just cause for objection? In Ryan's case, even if he wanted to co-operate, when he is feeling anxious, angry and upset he cannot sleep. He could lie quietly in his bed in the dark with his uncomfortable feelings – but is this reasonable? Would an adult do this, or would they get up, make a drink and maybe seek out someone to talk to?

This brings us on to **collaboration**. Adults will need to involve children in the process of deciding whether a request or expectation is reasonable. From this point the child (increasingly with age) needs to be involved in the process of problem solving, finding a solution to the mutually recognized problem. Ryan's inability to sleep is not only a problem for his parents; it is also a problem for him. He has unhappy bedtimes and feels tired and unwell in the morning, making it even harder to face the challenges of a new school. Finding a resolution will help Ryan also, although he may not immediately recognize this, so part of collaboration for younger children is careful explanation and guidance.

Finally Kohn suggests that following on from collaboration, problems need solutions which involve children in them. With very young children an effective strategy can be to offer two alternative **choices**, both of which is a better option for the adult than the status quo – but the child also feels that

Casey

Involve the child with finding a solution to the problem eg. by giving him a Choice

(r)

they have participated and have not been coerced. Ryan is old enough to enter into reasonably complex decisions about solutions; the outcome need not be as stark as either 'go to bed on time' or 'not go to bed on time'. A greater level of participation could be set up by saying, for example: 'I notice that in the mornings you are overtired. I have some ideas that might help you. Do you have any ideas that would help you be bright in the morning – ready for school?' This starting point could open up suggestions such as 'Would you like to go up to bed now and have 10 minutes looking at books with your light on, or would you like to play a game with Mummy for 10 minutes and then go straight to bed and lights out?' This does not guarantee that there will not still be some 'bartering', but it sets out a 'deal' in which Ryan may feel he has been given an option, even if the end result of both is 'lights out in 10 minutes'.

ACTIVITY 20	**WHO MAKES DECISIONS?**

Allow about 10 minutes

Drawing on experiences you have had as a child, as a parent or from general observations, make a list of the day-to-day practical decisions which adults commonly expect to make on behalf of children of Ryan's age.

COMMENT

How did you get on? If you are a parent, you may have reflected on any differences between the expectations of your parents and yourself as a parent. I listed the following decisions which are commonly thought of as being the responsibility, at least to some degree, of parents or guardians:

- food and meal routines
- clothes worn
- how much and what TV is watched
- bedtimes
- pocket money
- health treatment and/or medication.

Children's right to be involved in decision making

While it may not be too difficult to identify the areas of children's lives over which parents or other adults make decisions for them, it can be more difficult to explain why this is justified. One perspective of childhood is that children do not have sufficient understanding to make important decisions which affect their welfare. The difficulty with this argument, however, is that children gain competence in decision making as they are given opportunities to take part in matters that affect their lives. The other problem with this argument is that although a child may not have sufficient understanding to bear the responsibility solely of making important decisions, this does not mean that they should be excluded from the decision making process.

The difficulty with setting specific age restrictions on what children are allowed to do is that children mature and develop at different rates. This fact was recognized in UK courts as a result of the case of Gillick v West Norfolk and Wisbech Area Health Authority (1985). This court hearing made a judgement on the competence of children to make decisions relating to medical treatment which may be contrary to their parent's or guardian's wishes. It ruled that:

> As a matter of law the parental right to determine whether or not their minor child below the age of 16 will have medical treatment terminates if and when the child achieves sufficient understanding and intelligence to enable him to understand fully what is proposed.

This ruling is referred to as 'Gillick competence' and is used as a measure of whether a child below the age of 16 should be able to make important decisions. Since this ruling, laws in the UK increasingly reflect the notion that the ability to understand and make informed decisions is more important than chronological age.

Underlying this ruling is the assumption that for children under the age of 16 there is an expectation that parents have both the right and the responsibility to make important decisions about children's welfare. Returning to the list you made in Activity 20, these are probably the kind of day-to-day decisions which may seem trivial but relate to the child's welfare and are very important for children. Children may not want or have the capacity to take full responsibility for important decisions, but they do want to be involved and consulted. This involvement is also an important way in which children can gain experience so that when they do take full responsibility they have developed their abilities in decision making.

While parents may often ponder on how to persuade children to follow their advice, do you think that they also reflect upon the experience for children of having decisions made for them?

Effective study   Reading for study

The reading activity in Unit 1 illustrated that the experience of reading is different for all of us and many of us could learn to read more effectively for specific purposes. When you are reading for study it is important that you are extracting the information you need from your reading. You may find that much of the reading in front of you is not relevant for what you are doing at the time. It is also important that your reading does not become a passive process of reading word by word but not thinking or making any sense of what you are reading. So, your reading needs to be active and purposeful.

ACTIVITY 21	THE LITTLE TRIALS OF CHILDHOOD

Allow about 30 minutes

Imagine that you are collecting information for an essay about children's experiences of not being listened to or having their views taken into account.

Read the following extract, which is from a book by Frances Waksler (an American sociologist) who was interested in the everyday experiences of children.

Read through the extract twice. On the first read just skim fairly quickly to get an idea of the content. On the second read, highlight or make notes on any points which are relevant to the question:

• Are children listened to and are their views taken into account?

What are the little trials of childhood?

What kinds of experiences are described as difficulties, struggles, troubles and problems of childhood? Holly, for example, speaks of 'all the numerous times adults made my decisions for me,' and Sally writes,

> When I look back at my childhood, I can easily think of many experiences that I consider especially difficult. As I made a list of all the specific experiences that came to mind, I noticed they seemed to fall into three main categories. One category includes those experiences where I became fearful of a situation. The second category includes experiences where I felt a need to be accepted by my peers but was unable to because of parental control. Finally, the third category includes situations where an adult would not believe me although I was telling the truth.

Adults' claims that such experiences are trivial, even when adults are reflecting on their very own childhood, can obscure the experiences as they were lived. Pam writes of herself and her informants,

> The kinds of experiences I have identified are not ones that adults would necessarily characterize as hard for children. As one of my respondents noted, 'The experiences that I have told all seem so trivial now, like it was ridiculous to even have worried about them. But at the time they were so real, so important to me.'

As a way of demonstrating the non-trivial nature of these experiences, I offer a pair of stories. The first is what I see as a particularly clear example of an experience that might be viewed as fundamentally serious and non-trivial in adults' terms as well as in the terms of the teller.

> Something that really hurt when I was a child was when my grandfather was sick in the hospital. My father said I could go visit my grandfather. I got all ready to go and then my mother called and said I could not visit him. She said I was too young and could not handle it. But she did not understand how much I really wanted to see him, no matter what he looked like. I wanted to tell him I loved him and how much he meant to me. To this day it still hurts because I really wanted to let him know how I felt. (Inez)

Adults might readily term this story a description of a childhood trial. The story is not, however, in its manifest aspect, typical of the data I collected. I sought, and indeed found, far more manifestly ordinary data, but analysis had lead me to question this 'ordinary' aspect. Consider the following, apparently trivial, tale.

In my second year of preschool I had a few problems. I remember drawing a picture of my family. When it came time to draw my father I couldn't remember if a moustache was over or under the nose. I was too embarrassed to ask anyone, so I think I put it over his nose. In the same year I had a 'homework assignment' where I had to colour in some people. I asked my mom what colour do I colour in the people's face? She said, 'Red,' so I did. The next day I was laughed at by my teacher and my classmates because faces are not red, they should be orange. (Carol)

I myself smiled when I first read this story but the more I reread it in the course of the examining my data, the more I empathized with Carol's feeling of incompetence, her sense of 'no way out,' the embarrassment of one in this predicament. In all the stories I gathered there is an element of seriousness for the participants that remains even in the face of others' amusement, trivialization, or denial.

The little trials of childhood may have many sources. Some of the stories I present describe roles played by siblings and other children while other stories cite social structural sources, e.g., poverty in general, lack of money, and lack of opportunities. The prominence in what follows of adults as sources of childhood trials is not intended to minimize the importance of other sources but simply reflects my particular interest in adult–child interactions.

(Waksler, 1996, pp. 2–4)

COMMENT

Did you note down any points relevant to the question about children's views? Waksler offers us the examples of children not being allowed to visit a grandfather in hospital or forgetting where to draw a moustache on a face in pre-school. As you read you may have been thinking that you did not have these experiences, but may have had your own which you remember made you feel equally embarrassed or upset. One common experience children have is not being allowed to go to relatives' funerals as adults feel it will be too upsetting. Meal times are also a common source of painful memories, whether at home or at school, and many children also endure difficult experiences in physical education lessons at school.

Study note

Throughout *Understanding Children* you are given questions in some form to help you focus you reading. Each section will begin with over-arching core questions and when you come across specific reading activities you will be asked to think about or make notes on particular questions. This is a good habit to get into and one which you should be able to apply to any piece of reading as you move through your studies – although you will eventually need to start posing your own questions.

The subject matter of the previous activity may have touched a few nerves for you. Some adults, however, seem able to distance themselves from childhood experiences which may have been uncomfortable, upsetting or enraging at the time, accepting them as 'just the way things were'. Despite the fact that many children accept their lack of power in relation to adults, or find ways to evade the restrictions placed on them or negotiate alternatives with carers, others suffer and remember the 'trials' Waksler describes. Memories, such as spending hours toying with congealed food that needs to be eaten before leaving the table, may stay with us and influence our own parenting behaviour or eating patterns as adults. While such experiences range from insignificant to those verging on abusive, they have in common with each other the fact that they are markers of adults' power over children. Children are dependent on parents and carers to make just decisions on their behalf, and in providing the child some autonomy and choice.

HAPPIER BEDTIMES

Over the next two weeks Jodie took up Rosalind's offer and spent more time with Ryan on his own. They spent some time playing together but also started a new routine, with Jodie giving Ryan a bath, reading a story to him and having a cuddle before bed. This was not easy to organize – but Jodie and Eamon decided to keep Mia awake in the afternoon so that she slept through the night from 8:00 pm and was not competing for Ryan's attention. Just spending this time with Ryan seemed to help him settle, but he also began gradually telling Jodie that he had felt left out since Mia was born and hated going off to school, leaving her at home with Grandma and Pops. He didn't want to grow into a big boy and found school difficult, although he enjoyed his friends. Ryan also worried that he might be sent away to live with Graham now Jodie and Eamon had a new baby. He loved his daddy, but did not want to leave home. He felt special when he was at his daddy's and enjoyed staying up late – but was worried that he would get into trouble if Jodie or Eamon found out.

Ryan's bedtimes gradually changed from nightly battles to a special time which Ryan looked forward to. The 'chats with mum' soon ceased to be a way of 'solving a problem' for Jodie, and became an important space for her to devote some time to Ryan on his own. Keeping this time special was never easy, and did not always happen with competing demands from the rest of the Family, but it remained a part of the Family routine.

1.4 CONCLUSION

In this section we have followed Jodie's and Eamon's journey as they explored different ways of responding to solving a problem with Ryan. They began in a not uncommon position of seeing Ryan's behaviour as the problem. In seeking advice on possible ways to respond to his 'behaviour' they discovered a spectrum of responses from at one end smacking, which represents an extreme example of imposing adult will and power over a child, through to more collaborative approaches.

? for Emma
Behaviourism

Behaviourism, while still focusing on the child's behaviour as 'the problem', uses less overt coercion and relies to some extent on the child's thinking processes to work out the most advantageous behaviours in order to get positive responses from adults. This approach remains embedded in the assumption that adults have the right to decide what behaviours need to be changed, and as such still represents an exercise of power over the child. Some supporters of behaviourism do attempt to involve children in negotiating which behaviours need to change and the behavioural plan to achieve this.

Finally Jodie and Eamon came across the ideas of Alfie Kohn who directly challenges the imbalance of power between children and adults. Kohn is not alone in his views and his approach is not uncommon. Therapists working with distressed children have for many years been developing understanding of how to help children communicate their feelings, and increasingly psychologists are working in a similar way through supporting teachers in school. Kohn's ideas also fit well with increasing recognition of children's rights.

Key points

- While adults may need to take a lead in resolving family conflict, behavioural methods such as star charts as well as direct communication are more effective where young children are involved.
- Adults should not underestimate the significance of experiences such as family change and starting school on young children.
- Helping young children share their feelings requires patience, the ability to see things through children's eyes and some detective skills!

2   NEGOTIATIONS AT SCHOOL

CORE QUESTIONS

- What are the expectations of children as they start school?
- How do children experience the changes in expectations and routines as they move between home and school?
- How are young children's voices heard in school?

2.1 MOVING FROM HOME TO SCHOOL

The transition into the reception class in school is a major change for children. It is the point at which for many children the expectations and values that they have absorbed at home are first challenged. Children such as Ryan will not only be an individual but will also become a part of several 'groups' – class groups, sets within classes and members of 'infants'. They will also become objects of testing and assessment intended to measure both children's individual abilities and the performance of the school. This section will explore some of Ryan's experiences of his first year of formal education.

Beyond the introductory information in the case study you do not know much about Ryan's abilities. You do know, however, that he is four years old. All children are individual and different in some ways, but as they grow they also develop abilities which are broadly expected at certain life stages. These broad expectations are sometimes measured and recorded using a **developmental chart**. These charts divide children's development into categories which represent different areas of development such as **physical** (how they use their bodies), **self-help** (what they can do for themselves as they become more independent), **cognitive** (learning and understanding), and finally, **language and communication**.

| ACTIVITY 22 | WHAT IS EXPECTED OF A FOUR-YEAR-OLD? |

Allow about 15 minutes

Try to imagine a 'typical' four-year-old and think about what you would expect them to be able to do. Using your own experience and imagination, tick in the last column of the table below the things you would expect such a child to be able to do in terms of the categories 'physical', 'self-help' and 'language and communication'.

Table 10 What should four-year-olds be able to do?

Area of development	Measure of ability	Are most four-year-olds able to do this?
Physical	Walks downstairs using alternate feet	☑
	Hops on alternate feet	☑
	Throws ball overhand	☑
	Walks on a balance beam	☑
Self-help	Can dress without using simple fastenings	☑
	Can use buttons and zippers	☑
	Can use a knife and fork	☑
	Can use the toilet independently	☑
	Prepares a simple snack, such as a sandwich	☑
Language and communication	Enjoys stories and can answer simple questions	☑
	Can form complex sentences of more than 7 words	☑
	Pronunciation is mostly clear; may have some difficulties with *v*, *th* and *r* sounds	☑
	Understands prepositions (a cat, the dog, my house etc.)	☑

COMMENT

There is no absolute right or wrong for this activity as children vary so much. This is one reason why people involved in working with and researching children are cautious of terms such as 'normal' and 'average'. Just to give you an idea, however, I have filled in a copy of the chart you have just looked at with the age range during which most children would be developing each ability.

Table 11 Age range of development

Area of development	Measure of ability	Age range
Physical	Walks downstairs using alternate feet	4–5 years
	Hops on alternate feet	5–6 years
	Throws ball overhand	4–5 years
	Walks on a balance beam	5–6 years
Self-help	Can dress without using simple fastenings	3–4 years
	Can use buttons and zippers	4–5 years
	Can use a knife and fork	4–5 years
	Can use the toilet independently	3–4 years
	Prepares a simple snack, such as a sandwich	5–6 years
Language and communication	Enjoys stories and can answer simple questions	3–4 years
	Can form complex sentences of more than 7 words	5–6 years
	Pronunciation is mostly clear; may have some difficulties with *v*, *th* and *r* sounds	4–5 years
	Understands prepositions (*near* my house, *on* a bus, *with* a cat)	$4\frac{1}{2}$–$5\frac{1}{2}$ years

2.2 CHALLENGING EXPECTATIONS

The information in developmental charts like Table 11 is based upon the expected average development of 'normal' children growing up in a relatively affluent society. This means that expectations do not reflect children growing up with insufficient food, in dangerous living conditions without protection and stimulation by secure carers. They also do not take account of children who have physical or mental impairments or are exceptionally able in a particular area. In reality there are many factors which influence the way in which children grow, learn and develop social skills. Some of these factors will be to do with the environment where the child lives and the way in which people respond to the child. However, children will also differ naturally, either due to individual variations in abilities or due to impairments or disabilities which they are born with. Such differences do not make children 'abnormal' but represent the wide spectrum of development from which an average is drawn. So the description of the 'typical' or 'average' child can be misleading, as most children will not be 'typical'.

What makes four-year-olds different?

There are many factors which influence how children grow up, and developmental charts used in practice are careful to talk in terms of 'ranges' of ages when certain areas of development are expected. Even height and weight charts used to measure normal growth present upper and lower points of a range of expected normal growth. On the charts in Activity 23 the top edge of the tinted band indicates the maximum expected height/weight of an 'average' child and the bottom edge shows the minimum expected height/ weight of an 'average' child. On these charts we have also drawn in Ryan's actual height and weight between his birth and his fourth birthday.

While these charts are used to monitor children's growth against a broad 'average', there is only concern when children move outside of these upper and lower limits or if there is a sudden change in growth over a short period of time.

Effective study   Collecting and using evidence

The evidence which you can use for your essays can come from many different sources, just as research draws upon different sources. Charts and statistics can appear very convincing sources and may appear to offer more reliable 'facts' than research presented as a discussion or case study. All evidence, however, is open to scrutiny and criticism, and numerical evidence is as likely to be misleading or biased (or in other words presenting a one-sided or misleading view) as any other source of evidence.

| ACTIVITY 23 | LOOKING AT RYAN'S GROWTH |

Allow about 15 minutes

Have a look at the following growth charts which have Ryan's development marked on them. On the top chart the vertical line (marked 0–25) indicates the child's weight in kilograms. The horizontal line (marked birth–48) indicates the child's age in months. On the lower chart, the vertical line indicates the child's height in centimetres. The tinted band on both charts illustrates the expected normal range of height/weight for a child at each age. The line on each chart maps out Ryan's actual growth. Any child whose growth line moves outside the tinted area would be considered to be outside of the average or normal range and would possibly cause concern to healthcare professionals.

- Can you pick out any points on either of his charts when Ryan's growth might have caused concern?
- Taking into account both of the charts, do you think that a health visitor would have been worried?
- Do you see any problems with using this kind of evidence of growth?

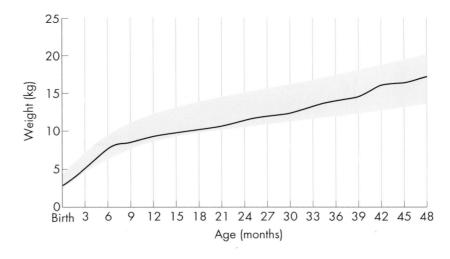

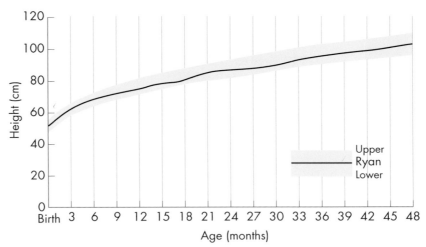

Figure 25 Ryan's growth charts

COMMENT

Ryan's growth has been pretty average; the only point at which his development may have caused concern was when he was born and then again between the ages of 18 months and 2 years when his weight dipped to the lower limit of the normal range.

A health professional would be unlikely to be concerned, however, as his height chart has remained steady and his weight has not dipped below the lower end of the average range or very suddenly. There are many possible reasons for his dip in weight at 18 months, including a growth spurt (his height does increase a little more sharply at about the same time) or a change in diet as he moves over to a fully solids diet.

Growth charts have been influenced by a particular view of child development. Averages are drawn from measurements of children's growth in a particular place, Western Europe, at a particular time. Although the averages have been adapted to try to take account of changes in culture and population, they still represent a questionable measure of healthy growth.

All of these ways of measuring development, including Ryan's growth chart, have been influenced by the assumption that development takes place *within* the child as a natural process. This is not the only view about how children grow and learn. A very different perspective is offered by Lev Vygotsky, a Russian psychologist. Vygotsky suggested that an individual child's development could be better understood by looking at the *environment* in which she or he grows up. The environment includes the social relationships (such as the child's family and friends), the culture in which the child grows up, and also the way in which the child sees herself or himself. All of these influences will be specific not only to the place where each child lives but also to a particular time in history when the child is growing up. For example, the expected development of a wealthy child growing up in Victorian England with high aspirations would be different from a child living at the same time but as an orphan in poverty. Similarly, in comparison with Victorian children there would be differences in expectations of children growing up in twenty-first century Britain, regardless of wealth and family circumstances. Expectations would be different again for children growing up in different circumstances across the world at different points in history.

This view challenges the idea that there are standard measures of development which are based on the 'natural' or 'normal' way in which humans grow from babies into adults. These have mostly been based upon scientific measures of average development of children in Western countries at a particular point in time. This means that children all over the world are being measured against an average child of specific social, cultural and economic contexts which are not representative of all children (Open University, 2002, pp. 113–14).

Vygotsky's model of development provides us with a more helpful way of understanding all children's experiences as they grow. It recognizes the significance of not only differences in children but also differences in the relationships which they have with other people such as parents and carers and their expectations.

Figure 26 Rebecca

This model would provide a more searching way of understanding Rebecca's development, for example. Rebecca is a five-year-old who has Down's syndrome. Being born with Down's syndrome does not result in predictable physical impairments; Rebecca may have the ability to develop the physical skills to, for example, fasten her own shoes along with her peers. However, over-protective attitudes or low expectations of her parents may result in help always being given, denying Rebecca the opportunity to develop new skills. Her development therefore is being limited not by the effects of her having Down's syndrome, but by the environment and relationships around her. A change in the over-protective care of her parents could enable Rebecca to develop new skills. Rebecca illustrates that for any child it can be more helpful to assess development on the basis of her own individual abilities in the context of her social relationships rather than assessing her development against a standard measure.

| ACTIVITY 24 | REASONS FOR DIFFERENCE |

Allow about 15 minutes

Have another look at the completed developmental chart (Table 11) in Activity 22. Try to think of as many reasons as you can for why children's abilities may differ from each indicator of development. Try to be specific and to include factors that are to do with the 'social context' and the environment in which the child lives as well as a child's individual differences. 'Social context' here refers to the child's culture including influences of social class, and the influences of family and the local community in which the child lives.

COMMENT

How did you get on? You may have found that one 'reason' may have an impact on many areas of development. For example, poverty leading to an inadequate diet could have an impact on not only physical growth but also on the development of concentration. The lack of secure and consistent parental relationships equally could have an impact upon physical development as well as the development of independence and confidence. A child with a particular physical impairment may develop more slowly in certain areas of physical development, either because of the impairment itself or as a result of the expectations of other people around the child or the restrictions of the environment in which the child lives.

2.3 EXPECTATIONS IN SCHOOL

Although we can see from this discussion that being different is in fact normal, on reception into compulsory education children begin to be measured against standard criteria. This takes place through assessment against six areas of learning which children are measured against throughout their pre-school and reception class. This period is called the 'Foundation Stage' and is intended to prepare children for beginning the National Curriculum in Year 1.

RYAN'S DEVELOPMENT

At the end of Ryan's first term Jodie and Eamon were invited to meet Ryan's reception class teacher, Mrs Dee, to discuss his development and needs. Mrs Dee also spoke to Graham when he collected Ryan one Friday. When they met, Mrs Dee shared with them a report sent on from Ryan's nursery. Mrs Dee explained the six areas of learning to them and told them that she would talk to Ryan so that his views were also reflected in the assessment. This gave them the opportunity to sit down together and think about Ryan's development, which had never caused any particular concern. Jodie had only considered his development when the time had come for his developmental checks with the health visitor or GP. Apart from these developmental reviews as a baby, at 2 years and at 3 years six months, Ryan had had little contact with the health services.

Effective study   Evaluating ideas

We have talked about study involving using your own ideas and also about the importance of using evidence. The reason that these are so important is that you will need to use both in order to develop an argument. As you saw in Unit 1, the word 'argument' as used in the context of studying doesn't mean an angry or emotional exchange. Rather, it is about presenting different viewpoints dispassionately – as the writer you are expected to be able to write about more than one point of view fairly. This is a skill which takes some practice and you will not be expected to do so well until you move beyond the first one or two years of your studies, but that is no reason for not beginning to practise now.

| **ACTIVITY 25** | **RYAN'S FOUNDATION STAGE PROFILE** |

Allow about 15 minutes

Have a look at this extract based on Ryan's Foundation Stage profile which was sent to Jodie and Eamon by Ryan's reception teacher. There are in fact six areas of learning, and 117 assessment points in total. These are the assessment points in the section headed 'Communication, language and literacy'.

You will need to think yourself into the shoes of three different people:
• the teacher who will complete the assessment
• the child
• the child's parents.

What would each of these think about this assessment? Note down your ideas.

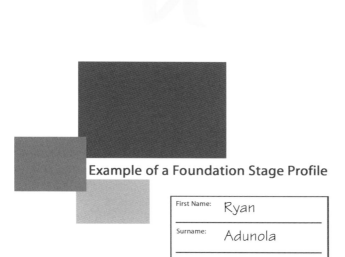

Example of a Foundation Stage Profile

First Name:	Ryan
Surname:	Adunola
Date of Birth:	1 5 0 6 9 9
	day month year
Gender:	Boy / Girl

Figure 27 Part of a Foundation Stage profile

Information about the child from previous settings

Ryan joined reception full time in September. He has been attending Springbank Nursery part time for one year. Records have been transferred. Ryan has settled well and is an outgoing and confident child. He is used to separating from his carers and is a lively and enthusiastic pupil.

Ryan's parents and stepfather all describe him as a confident and lively child who enjoys learning and stimulation. His mother and stepfather have had concerns about his sleep patterns and behaviour, but this appears to be resolved. Ryan also has a wonderful imagination and enjoys playing with his baby sister.

Discussion with child

Ryan enjoys 'playing with my friends and outdoor play'. He finds 'sitting quietly' quite hard and prefers free play and discussions. Ryan also says he does not like lunchtime or using the school toilets.

…

Communication, language and literacy

Reading

Points 4 to 8 are derived from the early learning goals and can be achieved in any order.

1 Is developing an interest in books. ☑
2 Knows that print conveys meaning. ☐
3 Recognises a few familiar words. ☐
4 Knows that, in English, print is read from left to right and top to bottom. ☐

5   Shows an understanding of the elements of stories, such as main character, sequence of events and openings. ☑

6   Reads a range of familiar and common words and simple sentences independently. ☐

7   Retells narratives in the correct sequence, drawing on language patterns of stories. ☑

8   Shows an understanding of how information can be found in non-fiction texts to answer questions about where, who, why and how. ☐

9   Reads books of own choice with some fluency and accuracy. ☐

Comments

Ryan is keen on stories but needs to develop more familiarity with books and writing.

Writing

Points 4 to 8 are derived from the early learning goals and can be achieved in any order.

1   Experiments with mark-making, sometimes ascribing meaning to the marks. ☑

2   Uses some clearly identifiable letters to communicate meaning. ☑

3   Represents some sounds correctly in writing. ☑

4   Writes own name and other words from memory. ☐

5   Holds a pencil and uses it effectively to form recognisable letters, most of which are correctly formed. ☐

6   Attempts writing for a variety of purposes, using features of different forms. ☐

7   Uses phonic knowledge to write simple words and make phonetically plausible attempts at more complex words. ☐

8   Begins to form captions and simple sentences, sometimes using punctuation. ☐

9   Communicates meaning through phrases and simple sentences with some consistency in punctuating sentences. ☐

Language for communication and thinking

Points 4 to 8 are derived from the early learning goals and can be achieved in any order.

1   Listens and responds. ☑

2   Initiates communication with others, displaying greater confidence in more informal contexts. ☑

3   Talks activities through, reflecting on and modifying actions. ☑

4   Listens with enjoyment to stories, songs, rhymes and poems, sustains attentive listening and responds with relevant comments, questions or actions. ☑

5 Uses language to imagine and recreate roles and experiences. ☑

6 Interacts with others in a variety of contexts, negotiating plans and activities and taking turns in conversation. ☐

7 Uses talk to organise, sequence and clarify thinking, ideas, feelings and events, exploring the meanings and sounds of new words. ☐

8 Speaks clearly with confidence and control, showing awareness of the listener. ☐

9 Talks and listens confidently and with control, consistently showing awareness of the listnerby including relevant detail. Uses language to work out and clarify ideas, showing control of a range of appropriate vocabulary. ☐

Linking sounds and letters

Points 4 to 8 are derived from the early learning goals and can be achieved in any order.

1 Joins in with rhyming and rhythmic activities. ☑

2 Shows an awareness of rhyme and alliteration. ☑

3 Links some sounds with letters. ☐

4 Links sounds to letters, naming and sounding letters of the alphabet. ☑

5 Hears and says initial and final sounds in words. ☐

6 Hears and says short vowel sounds within words. ☐

7 Uses phonic knowledge to read simple words. ☐

8 Attempts to read more complex words, using phonic knowledge. ☐

9 Uses knowledge of letters, sounds and words when reading and writing independently. ☐

COMMENT

I thought that some teachers may feel insulted by this assessment. They may feel that they are able to make an assessment of each child's progress without having to fill in 180 tick boxes. I also thought the teacher might feel that spending time on the profiles would reduce the time they had to spend teaching the children.

I don't imagine that many children will even know that the profiles exist. They may see them briefly when the teacher asks for their views, but generally I would expect that teachers would seek children's views in a more informal way, rather than sitting down with a large form.

I thought some parents might feel reassured by the profile. It gives them some evidence that their child is being assessed against standard guidelines and treated as an individual. I also thought parents would welcome their views being recorded.

Of course, we are only guessing about what parents, children and teachers *might* think about the profiles; this is not the same thing as providing evidence. If you were using these views in an essay to build an argument then you would need to find some evidence to support them. This exercise does give you a taster, however, of how the same subject can be viewed very differently by different people.

You will see from Ryan's profile that he has received a tick against most of points 1–3 and some of points 4–8, although not in any order. This form of assessment recognizes that children will not develop at the same rate and will have areas of strength or delay in different areas. Ryan's

Figure 28 Ryan with Mrs Dee

family experiences mean that he is already confident in playing with other children and has a very good understanding of difference and cultures, which other children may not have at his age. The profile also provides an opportunity for Mrs Dee to meet with Ryan and his parents to ask them about their thoughts and ideas about how Ryan is getting on.

Both this form and the developmental charts discussed above imply that there is a standard or level that children are expected to meet at certain ages. Failing to meet these expectations, particularly when your child is about to move from the private environment of the family and into the very public world of the school, could feel quite threatening. The Foundation Stage profile is not, in fact, a set of expectations, but a tool for reception teachers to measure children's progress towards national levels of achievement by the end of their first year. Such information is also useful for teachers in the process of getting to know children new to the school and sending a message to parents about the kinds of expectations which will be made of their children.

Testing and assessment

By the age of five or the end of the reception year, all children are supposed to have attained a standard level of development in England which is prescribed by the foundation level in preparation for the National Curriculum. The introduction of standardized testing and assessment of children at the age of four to five has been hotly debated by educators and policy makers. Policy makers have supported the implementation of guidance for teachers to ensure that all children are measured against and supported to achieve standard levels of achievement in a range of areas. Critics of these developments, however, suggest that the introduction of formal curriculum education at such a young age can be unhelpful in that it focuses learning on narrow targets such as literacy rather than valuing play and exploration which, critics argue, develop broader skills and a sense of 'well being'. In addition it has been suggested that the Foundation Stage encourages competitiveness amongst children which supports those more likely to succeed (Open University, 2002, pp. 235–6).

The Foundation Stage is not only about assessment and setting targets for individual children. It also provides nursery and reception teachers with a framework around which to plan their teaching. The *early learning goals* (and *stepping stones*, the achievements that need to be attained before moving onto the early learning goals) are divided into six areas of learning:

- Personal, social and emotional development
- Communication, language and literacy
- Mathematical development
- Knowledge and understanding of the world
- Physical development
- Creative development.

| ACTIVITY 26 | OBSERVING A RECEPTION CLASS |

Allow about 20 minutes

DVD Band 4

DVD Band 4 was filmed at Shepherdswell First School in Milton Keynes. In the DVD you will see the reception class during part of a physical education lesson. You may want to watch the clip a couple of times, and should then note down:

- any examples of how Ann Green provides structure and formality to the lesson
- any examples of 'skills' you think that Ann Green might be trying to help the children develop.

COMMENT

What did you think about this reception lesson? Did it seem formal to you or did you feel that the atmosphere was fairly relaxed? Ann Green and her teaching assistant, Helen Lasenby, were certainly trying to help these children in their second week in reception to get used to the expectations of school. Did you notice that the children were already listening quietly as Ann Green spoke to them as a group, explaining the activity to them? The children were also able to work co-operatively with each other to take out the equipment and also to take turns on the apparatus.

The teacher and assistant in this clip could have developed the children's abilities in a number of areas of the early learning goals, and Ann Green says in the clip that these are planned into each lesson so that individual children have the opportunity to develop. I picked out that the children were being given an opportunity to develop confidence, concentration, balance, co-ordination and co-operation with others. These skills would help children achieve their early learning goals not only in physical development, but also in personal, social and emotional development as well.

The expectations of reception or nursery classes can be a shock for many children. The expectations of them at home which are so familiar will almost certainly be different in some ways. This is because children all come from very different families, with different ways in which they discipline, reward and communicate with children and also a great diversity of ways of life.

RYAN'S EXPERIENCE OF RECEPTION CLASS

Jodie and Eamon found their meeting with Mrs Dee helpful. The only concern it raised for them was Ryan's familiarity with books. Both Jodie and Eamon tell stories to their children; it is an important part of their family life to make up stories, and both Daisy and Ryan love this family activity and as a result are confident speakers with vivid imaginations. Daisy had moved into school with a similar lack of familiarity with books, but had taken to reading and writing stories very quickly. Ryan has a great enthusiasm for stories and learning and his comprehension and vocabulary are excellent, so they hope that he will also catch up quickly. They are also worried about Ryan's lively nature and how he will respond to being expected to sit quietly and listen as part of a group.

ACTIVITY 27   EXPECTATIONS OF THE RECEPTION CHILDREN

Allow about 10 minutes

Read the following short extract in which a reception teacher describes helping new children to settle into reception. What examples does this teacher give of expectations of independence and conformity?

> Very early on there are lots of sessions on the carpet, explaining how we do things, and I might notice that a few of the new ones obviously haven't grasped that they ask to go to the toilet and so on. So I'll just sit again and talk about that … I suppose my main job is about making them look after themselves, I think socially, or – yes, I do expect them to look after themselves.

(Mayall, 1996, p. 75)

COMMENT

Did you notice that this teacher uses the phrase 'how we do things'? By this the teacher is telling us that there is a shared expectation within the school about how the children should behave. It is unlikely that many children will have been used to asking to go to the toilet at home, unless they were asking for assistance. This will be a new expectation and the reception teacher here sees part of her role as being to 'socialize' the children into this behaviour in order to 'help them settle in'. The word 'socialize' here refers to the process through which people adopt common ways of behaving in order to fit in with those, or the society, around them.

What is it like to feel 'different' in a crowd?

Schools need children to conform in order to manage the co-existence of large numbers of children. But most children also have a strong desire to fit in, to melt into the crowd. From the age of four or five children are increasingly able to make choices about who they make friends with. Before the age of four children generally play alone, with adults, or 'alongside' rather than 'with' other children. This change in patterns of play is referred to as move from 'solitary' and 'parallel' play to 'co-operative' play. Solitary play means that the child plays alone, or with the help of an adult. Before they develop the skills to interact co-operatively with other children, they will play alongside others, perhaps even doing the same activity. As their social skills develop they will begin to interact with other children of their own age in shared activities.

ACTIVITY 28	**PLAY**

Allow about 10 minutes

DVD Band 5

DVD Band 5 includes clips of children involved in all three kinds of play. Watch the clip through and note down which you thought was which.

COMMENT

Did you spot which clip showed the children playing co-operatively with each other? They were not only engaged in the same activity but were talking and including each other in the play.

Who shall I play with?

Children are not unlike adults in that they select friends with whom they have something in common such as gender, social background and interests. Children who stand out as being significantly different from their peers may in fact find it harder to make friends, although a confident personality can overcome this. This differentiation of children who are identified as 'different' for any reason by a group of children explains in part why children belonging to any minority – such as belonging to a black or minority-ethnic group, wearing glasses or even being unusual looking – can find themselves subject to teasing, hostility or exclusion.

Negative attitudes towards children who appear to be different stem from the beliefs and attitudes that children learn at home and from the world around them. When children repeatedly see pictures and TV images of black and minority-ethnic people and disabled people, for example, presented in a stereotypical way, these misleading beliefs can take root and be acted out in school. Such images and stereotypes can be as simple as never seeing disabled people doing everyday jobs such as being doctors, builders or office workers. Stereotypes can, more importantly, be created by disabled people just not being part of children's everyday experiences as peers. Stereotypes of black and minority-ethnic people also remain common on TV and in advertisements portraying particular 'groups' as having common characteristics rather as individuals, such as African-Caribbean athletes and Middle Eastern terrorists.

'I have four-year-old identical twin boys and have had discussions with the primary school about them starting school this year. They felt it would be OK to put them in the same class, but they fight and bite a lot. The school has realized now that having them in separate classes would be the best idea! But like all children twins are different and some twins may need to be put in the same class to begin with or for all their school career.'

All schools have a responsibility to encourage children to value each other as individuals and to value the diverse cultures represented in many schools. They also are required to support children's emotional welfare and combat bullying, as you will read later in this section.

Individual differences

So, as Ryan is being socialized into school routines, he encounters some expectations which are new for many children, such as asking to go to the toilet, but he also encounters some expectations which seem odd or unreasonable only to him. Most of Ryan's classmates do not seem to want to join in with the story telling as much as he does, for example. This is because this particular expectation of conformity – to sit still and quietly, listen to the story, and only speak if a question is asked – may be very familiar to some children. These expectations do not reflect 'good' or 'bad' behaviour, but culturally specific ways of enjoying stories. Ryan's family members share a tradition of oral story telling. For other children text- or book-based stories which are read aloud are familiar and carry with them comfortable expectations of quiet listening. An approach which enables children to begin developing listening and literacy skills can be interwoven with encouraging imaginative participation through talking and acting out stories.

Let us take a few examples of the ways Ryan had to adapt in his first term of reception class.

RYAN'S THOUGHTS ABOUT SCHOOL

Ryan:

I hate using the toilets at school. When I first saw them I thought they were silly and tiny weenie and they had a wall to wee into! I hate that – everyone can see your privates – even in the toilet the teachers can look over the top. It's embarrassing. I can use a big toilet on my own – I don't even need Mum to help me – these look like baby toilets. But what I really hate is the smell, and the yucky scratchy toilet paper and people watching you. And the worst thing as well is that you have to put your hand up and ask the teacher if you can go – so everyone knows! I try to hold on until I get home – if I don't have a big drink I usually can do it.

Figure 29 Primary school children's toilets

Ryan:

I love story time!!! – but the stories are never as good as Eamon or Auntie Rosalind tell – they let me be the animals and monsters and to help make up the story. I can ROAR like the lions and jump like the monkeys and everything. Mrs Dee doesn't like me doing that. She always says 'Sit nicely Ryan' and she sounds cross when she asks us, 'What happened next, children?' and I make up

Figure 30 Story time at school

a more exciting ending, she says, 'That's nice Ryan, but can you remember what happens in this story?' She's never as pleased with me as Auntie Rosalind!

Ryan:

I hate lunchtime. I can never open my lunchbox and we are supposed to do it on our own so the helper looks cross with me. And my drink lid is really hard. Sometimes I think that my drink will spill in my bag. The other kids always eat faster than me – just like Daisy does at home. But at home it is different because we all eat at the kitchen table and it is always mad – with Mia making a noise and a big mess, everyone talking and me and Daisy messing – that's what Eamon says anyway. I like eating at home; I can get my own yoghurt and spoon and sometimes I help Mia eat her mush. We all take ages at home, not just me. You don't have to hurry up like at school so they can clear the hall for the juniors. Mum keeps grumping because I don't eat all my food and am hungry when I get home. I don't know if she is mad with me or not.

Figure 31 School meals

ACTIVITY 29   IN RYAN'S SHOES

Allow about 10 minutes

Spend ten minutes thinking about Ryan's experiences in school. They are not particularly uncommon or resulting from Ryan having any unusual needs. Why do you think Ryan might be experiencing these difficulties? Can you think of any possible solutions to make Ryan's experiences in school happier?

COMMENT

How did you get on? You may have memories similar to Ryan's experience of the strangeness of the school environment; maybe you can still remember the smell and noises of school which can be so evocative of childhood experiences. Ryan, along with many children, reacted to the unfamiliar environment of school but he also was confronted by facilities and expectations which, if he had been an adult, would have given him good reason for complaint about the service he was receiving. The toilets were unpleasant and lacked privacy. Story time did not allow him to feel that his family culture or his individuality was valued. Lunch arrangements, together with poor toilet facilities, resulted in Ryan being forced to make unhealthy lifestyle choices by skipping food and drinks. Changes to the physical environment, attitudes and routines could all help provide a happier and healthier environment for Ryan and his friends.

Adjusting to school

School is a very different environment from home for all children and requires some major adjustment. Some of the issues for Ryan will be common for many children, such as feelings about using the school toilets and getting used to different expectations at meal times. Ryan also experienced discomfort about different expectations of his behaviour which were culturally based. All families have a 'culture' or a set of common expectations and beliefs about how its members will behave and live together. These may be related to religion, nationality, heritage or just customs common to a particular family. For Ryan, story telling is an exciting, active and participatory family event which is based on made-up spoken stories rather than reading books. Entering a school culture with a strong focus on valuing written stories, Ryan could easily feel that his own family experiences were not being valued.

School toilets are designed to enable children to be independent but are also closely supervised by teachers. While both independence and safety are important, children have the same feelings about privacy as grown-ups and also value pleasant environments. Some public toilets for children in supermarkets now provide a good model for child-orientated facilities which are pleasant, private and easy to use.

Ryan's disappointment in story time illustrates the concerns discussed above about an over-concentration on literacy to the exclusion of less formal, more creative free play. Ryan's experience also raises the issue of the degree to which school provides a 'mono-cultural' environment in which the cultural tradition of literacy is valued to the exclusion of oral traditions which are valued in many cultures. While children will need to develop skills in literacy,

Figure 32 Good example of child-oriented facilities

this should not exclude the valuing and incorporation of oral stories; these can also develop important skills while also valuing the diversity of children's home experiences.

Ryan's hurried lunch breaks are an illustration of how a school's need for order and regimentation/structure can be detrimental to not only children's ability to be individual, but also potentially to health.

Independence and conformity

Schools are concerned with promoting independence in terms of children developing the skills to look after themselves to a greater degree than many have at home. Children are expected to quickly learn to 'line up' when prompted, to go to the toilet without assistance, to open their food and drink containers alone and to find their own coat peg. But such independence is within the context of conformity – children need to (independently) behave in the same way as their peers. Ryan is struggling with the new expectations of his independence – using the school toilets and managing his own lunch containers. But he is also meeting expectations of conformity which are new to him and often puzzling. Why is he not praised for adding new endings to the stories and acting out the monsters – behaviour which delights his family? Why does he have to rush his lunch when Jodie always says: 'Take your time Ryan – don't talk with your mouth full – tell us about your day!'

2.4 HEALTH IN SCHOOL: POLICY AND REALITY

CONCERNS ABOUT HEALTH AT SCHOOL

Jodie and Eamon are particularly concerned about Ryan's health at school. They have always believed in teaching the children to take responsibility for their own personal care and to think about their health. In practice this has meant that they talk to Ryan about healthy food, drinking plenty of water and about why cleaning his teeth is important. Talking with Ryan about his problems with eating enough lunch, Jodie also finds out that Ryan is not allowed to clean his teeth after his lunch and that he can only have a drink of squash with their biscuit, provided by the school, at break and his own bottle of water at lunchtime. In addition Ryan's anxiety over the toilets is resulting in him not drinking enough.

Concerns about children's health in school have been acknowledged in the publication of the national Healthy Schools Standard in 1999 (DfEE, 1999). This government policy encourages schools to develop local plans to address eight key areas (personal, social and health education; citizenship; drug education; emotional health; healthy eating; physical activity; safety; sex and relationships education). This initiative also encourages schools to actively involve not only parents but also children through forums such as school councils.

Despite government concern for children's health in principle, applying healthy eating to the routines of school can be challenging. Research carried out to investigate children's experiences in primary schools identified that:

> Children faced certain contradictions within the formal and informal agendas and conditions of school. Health education messages might conflict with the physical and social conditions. Children who were overcrowded in class, and thought they needed more physical exercise, might be taught the merits of activity. Some children were faced with lavatories and wash basins which failed to measure up to hygiene messages and were almost certainly below the standards they lived with at home. And, notably, food provided at school was likely to include unhealthy components, judged by health education messages, and by family standards. The school as a health-promotion environment was faulty in important respects.

(Mayall, 1996, p. 212)

This research illustrates that, while schools may be actively teaching children about healthy living, the physical conditions and practices in many schools contradict these messages. Moreover, many children experience school as presenting a less healthy environment than they are used to at home.

The national guidance on the Healthy Schools Standard suggests that schools have a responsibility to take into account not only physical welfare but also emotional health including bullying. The national guidelines suggest that in order to achieve the Healthy Schools Standard:

> the school openly addresses issues of emotional health and well-being by enabling pupils to understand what they are feeling and by building their confidence to learn

(DfEE, 1999, p. 16)

One approach introduced in many primary schools committed to improving the emotional well-being of pupils is 'circle time'. While there are variations in how circle time is implemented, the following activity will give you a feeling for the approach.

ACTIVITY 30	CIRCLE TIME

Allow about 20 minutes

The following extract is from a book by Teresa Bliss which is intended to provide guidance for teachers and heads concerned about improving communication with and between children in schools. This section specifically deals with the benefits of 'circle time' in developing children's confidence in communicating with each other. Read through the extract and then, imagining that you are Ryan's teacher, note down three topics which you feel would help the class settle into their new environment and how you think each topic might help Ryan and his friends. Don't worry if you have over-lapping benefits for different topics.

Figure 33 Circle time at Cottesbrooke Infants School

Circle time

Many teachers work with their classes in a circle. However the focus here is on the children themselves rather than on curriculum issues. A class sits with the teacher in a circle using enjoyable 'games' and activities to foster self-esteem, develop sharing, co-operation, listening and speaking skills.

By being non-evaluative, accepting and sensitive the teacher shows he values the children and respects what they have to say.

This way of working nurtures peer relationships and group bonding within the class. Greater trust is built up, and of course self-esteem as children become more aware of themselves and each other through greater knowledge and responsibility.

Class groups that work in this way as part of a whole-school policy use circle time to develop self-discipline, generate determination, and greater individual autonomy. This is a gradual process linked to children's own emotional and cognitive processes and development.

(Bliss, 1994, p. 17–18)

COMMENT

While circle time is used differently in different schools and with different age groups, there are some common general rules or principles for circle time, for example:

- Everyone has a right to be heard and a duty to listen.
- There should be no 'put downs'. In the first stages it may be that the rule should be that all statements made should be positive.
- Everyone has the right to pass.
- Everything said should be confidential unless otherwise agreed.

Circle time can be used to counter a bullying subculture in a school. It might also be used to: help children gain insight into communicating with other people; help children gain and maintain mutual respect amongst peers; raise self-esteem through affirmation, understanding and support; develop positive discipline; give training in social skills, problem solving and conflict resolution. It has a wide range of applications in the school and work context for creating a friendly forum for any participant to discuss problems as and when they arise, and to develop resolution strategies and examine their effectiveness.

A similarly simple activity could involve asking each child to say how they feel today. This would also build confidence in speaking in a group but would also help children to learn to name their feelings and to develop trust and empathy amongst the class. The teacher's responsibility will be to ensure that children feel emotionally safe in such a group and also to help children find words to express themselves. This last topic could be a good way to open up broader discussions such as the concerns that Ryan has about the school toilets, dinner time or story time. You may have thought of setting these as topics – they would all develop children's confidence and skills in self-expression as well as possibly bringing about change in the school by providing a forum for their views to be heard.

Birmingham's Healthy Schools Standard

Birmingham is one example of a local education authority which has adopted the Healthy Schools Standard and published its own local guidelines encouraging schools to develop their own policies and apply for the award of the Birmingham Healthy Schools Standard. A 'healthy school' is defined in the guidance:

> A healthy school is one that is successful in helping pupils to do their best and build on their achievements. It is a school which has created an enjoyable, safe and productive learning environment. A healthy school is committed to continuous development through self review and promotes the ethos of achievement; of valuing each member of the community; and supporting the development of all pupils to make the most of their gifts, talents and abilities.

> (Birmingham Health Education Unit, 2000, p. 3)

This statement demonstrates that although the Healthy Schools Standard is concerned with the physical health and environment of the school (such as the toilets, provision of drinking water and nutrition) it is also concerned with the social and emotional well-being of children.

Figure 34 Cottesbrooke Infants School, Birmingham

Figure 35 Ann Phillips, head of Cottesbrooke Junior and Infant School, Birmingham

---

ACTIVITY 31   REMOVING BARRIERS TO LEARNING

Allow about 45 minutes

You will now need to find your course audio CD and listen to the recording of an interview with Ann Phillips, head of Cottesbrooke Junior and Infant School in Birmingham. We asked Ann about her experiences of putting the Birmingham Healthy Schools initiative into practice. You may want to listen to the recording a couple of times. As you listen, think about the following questions and jot down your answers:

- What is Cottesbrooke School doing to improve its pupils' health?
- Did you hear any examples of how the changes intended to improve the health of the children also made it easier for them to learn in the classroom?
- How were children given a say?

COMMENT

How did you get on? There is a lot of information on this audio recording; you may want to come back to it to gather evidence for your essays. Clearly Cottesbrooke is an excellent example of how the Healthy Schools initiative can be put into practice, and in fact the school was already making many positive changes to improve the health of its pupils. We noted down the following answers for the questions:

We were interested to hear that 'health' did not just mean physical health, such as diet and exercise. The school was also concerned about the emotional well-being of the children. Ann Phillips talked about the importance of making drinking water available throughout the day, a change which broke the routine of the lessons, but was soon accepted as a normal part of school life. We also noticed the ways in which the school had responded to children feeling unhappy during playtime. The 'friendship bench' was obviously well used and lunchtime assistants and playground buddies were involved in organizing games so that children did not feel left out.

Ann Phillips used the phrase 'barriers to learning' to refer to aspects of the children's welfare that she felt made it difficult for them to learn. The school nurse gave the example of dehydration making it difficult for the children to concentrate. She also mentioned research that had suggested that not drinking enough or using the toilet often enough increased the risk of urine infections for children. So the relatively small change of giving the children water in their classrooms both improved their physical health and their brainpower! We were also interested in Ann Phillips' recognition that unhappy playtimes were also a barrier to learning. When children returned from their breaks unhappy, anxious or angry it would take valuable learning time out of the lesson before they could be settled down.

We were pleasantly surprised that children as young as those in the reception class were fully involved in the forum set up to ask children their opinions about changes in the school. The children's wish for the playground to have a garden area with flowers was being taken seriously and being developed. Older children were also involved in going to the City Council House to present the school's plan and are involved in the regular schools council. Did you notice Ann Phillips saying that circle time was used in the school as another way in which children of all ages could have their say? They could, for example, tell their teachers if there was anything they were unhappy about or would like to change about the school.

Figure 36 Playtime at Cottesbrooke

Involving children

The importance of involving children in the Healthy Schools Standard is evident in two main ways. Firstly, the issues of health should be included in lessons to develop children's knowledge and awareness of health issues. Cottesbrooke School invited an artist into the school who made giant cut-out caricatures of healthy food! Secondly, children's views should contribute to the identification of targets intended to bring about improvements in the health of the school. We heard Ann Phillips tell us about the children's request for a garden to relax in during playtime. The Birmingham Healthy Schools Standard guidelines suggest each school should set up pupil 'focus groups' to ensure that pupils are involved in this planning process and as we heard at Cottesbrooke these focus groups involved children of all ages.

We were interested in finding out from children in the reception class at Cottesbrooke School how much they now understood about healthy lifestyles. We were also interested in their views about whether, if it was left up to them, they would follow healthy living guidelines, and how they felt about their parents having some control over their what they eat and how they look after their bodies.

ACTIVITY 32	THE VIEWS OF RECEPTION CHILDREN

Allow about 60 minutes

Listen to the following recording of a small group of children from Cottesbrooke reception class. They are having a mini circle time with one of their teachers, Alison Everette. You will hear Alison asking the children to 'pass Stripey'; Stripey is a toy tiger which the children need to hold when they want to speak, so that they learn to speak one at a time and listen to each other. Alison had asked the children to bring two pictures with them. The first was a picture of what they would most like to eat if they had a magic wish. The second was a picture of what they actually ate the previous day.

You may find that you need to work quite hard to hear and understand the children. They have not been rehearsed and listening to them should give you a very genuine experience of trying to listen to four and five year olds. You will need to find somewhere quiet and without distraction and concentrate hard as you listen. The transcript provided as part of your course materials may help here.

As you listen to the children, note down:

- any examples of what the children know about healthy living
- who the children say decides what they eat
- how you think the children felt about adults making decisions about healthy living for them.

COMMENT

Were you surprised by what these children said? They certainly did seem to have a good understanding of healthy living. We heard them mention eating fruit and vegetables, doing exercise and cleaning their teeth. They did not seem to mind eating fruit – in fact it was on several children's 'wish list', unlike vegetables! The children were unanimous that their parents or the dinner ladies decided what they should eat, despite the fact that they clearly had good knowledge themselves.

We were very interested in this last question. Although not quite so unanimous, the children did seem to think that it was OK for adults to guide their behaviour. No one objected to being told to clean his or her teeth. If you have children of your own, or know some children of this age or a little older, you might like to ask them the same questions. One of the authors asked her four and six year olds and got very similar answers. They were very clear about what they should do to keep healthy, but did not want the full responsibility of making sure that they did it. They did want choices and to be consulted, but had no objections to a guiding parental hand.

From this activity we can see that even very young children are able to understand the consequences of quite complex combinations of actions and also protective action that they can take. It is also clear, however, that children of this age feel that they need some help in keeping to healthy living behaviour which is contrary to what they really want!

Figure 37 Cottesbrooke Children and Stripey

2.5 CONCLUSION

Starting school will always be a challenging experience for children. It marks a major milestone in their gradual move from the familiarity of the home towards the complexity of negotiating different social relationships and expectations. It is also likely to be their first experience of a large organization which in order to operate effectively needs a degree of regulation and conformity. Within this context, however, schools recognize the importance of valuing diversity and promoting independence in children. In this section we have looked at health as just one example of how schools are attempting to involve and respond to the needs of the community, of parents and also of children. Children's voices are increasingly being heard not only through school councils and forums, but are being valued individually such as in the use of circle time.

Key points

- Although it is recognized that children differ greatly in their development, when they start school they begin to be assessed against standardized measures of achievement.

- School can be a culture shock for many children as they encounter the expectations of routine and regimentation perhaps for the first time.

- Even very young children's voices are increasingly being heard in schools through, for example, circle time, focus groups and school councils.

Effective study   Essay writing

In the previous 'Essay writing' entry you reflected on the kinds of writing that you are used to doing. When you begin to develop your writing for a new context or purpose, such as university courses, it is important to learn the 'rules of the game'. When you write for study there are some common rules which apply across most disciplines, but there will also be some expectations of how you write which are specific to your subject. In most subjects you will be expected to:

1   Write clearly using standardized grammar and punctuation.

2   Structure your answer using an introduction, paragraphs which build up your argument, and a conclusion.

3   Use evidence to support the points you are making.

4   Acknowledge the work of other people (such as published sources) used in your writing.

5   Build an argument, rather than merely describing or reproducing what you have studied.

The scope of this course does not allow the authors space to 'teach' writing for study comprehensively. The *effective study* topics of 'collecting and using evidence' and 'evaluating ideas' will introduce you to points 3, 4 and 5 respectively. If you feel that you need help with point 1, you could have a look at *Student Toolkit 1: The effective use of English* (Open University, 1999) or seek advice from your tutor. We will consider point 2 in Unit 3.

All of the above points contribute to creating writing expected in higher education and all of them may be very unfamiliar to the kinds of writing which you are used to. They may seem overwhelming now – but you are not expected to become an expert at all of them right away. Everyone involved in study and academic writing (not only students!) is continually practising and developing their writing, so think of it as a journey rather than a quick fix. Although you will only be getting feedback from your tutor on your two assignments, don't feel restricted by this – practise writing as often as you can. If someone can read your work and let you know whether they understood it, so much the better. You can use any of the core questions as mini-essay questions to practise your writing.

So, returning to learning the 'rules of the game', you know that there are likely to be some expectations of your writing but will need to check out exactly what these are. For any piece of assessed writing, therefore, you should stop and ask yourself the following three questions:

- *What* am I being asked to write – are there any written guidelines?
- *Who* am I writing for – who is my audience?
- What am I writing *about* – do I have some evidence and some ideas?

Stop here and have a look at your second assignment. This is your second opportunity to do some writing and get some feedback on it. Try to answer these three questions here.

Table 12 Rules of the game

What am I being asked to write – are there any written guidelines?	

Who am I writing for – who is my audience?	
What am I writing *about* – do I have some evidence and some ideas?	

Here are the ideas that we came up with.

Table 13 Rules of the game continued

What am I being asked to write – are there any written guidelines?	The assignment asks you to write an 'essay'. From this you can assume that you are expected to write using an academic structure (see 2 above) and that you should be using evidence (3), acknowledging your sources (4) and building an argument (5). There are also some specific guidelines for this course which relate to the way in which you use personal experience and writing using the first person ('I'). These expectations are not common on courses in other disciplines which might insist, for example, that you write impersonally. So instead of writing 'I have observed' you would need to write 'It has been observed'. In *Understanding Children* it is fine to use 'I', particularly when you are talking about your own experience.
Who am I writing for – who is my	Your essay will be read and assessed by your tutor, although for your first and second assignments the outcomes will not contribute towards your final

audience?	assessment. Your tutor is an individual in their own right with their own ideas and preferences, but they are also representing the course team who produce this course and in fact the wider University. As such they should be assessing your work along standardized guidelines, which you can read in your Assignment Booklet. It is always worth asking yourself what you think your tutor is looking for in your essays.
What am I writing *about* – do I have some evidence and some ideas?	This final section is to do with your subject – in this case *Understanding Children*. Even writing which keeps strictly to the rules of the discipline is pointless without content. You need to be showing your tutor that you have understood the subject and the question and have selected appropriate evidence and ideas. By 'appropriate' we mean that they should be relevant to the question, be explained in such as way as to show that you understand the subject and ideally put forward some kind of 'argument'.

ACTIVITY 33	EFFECTIVE STUDY REVIEW ACTIVITY

Complete this activity on a separate piece of paper and send it to your tutor as part A of assignment 2.

We hope that the six areas of *effective study* are beginning to make some sense to you now. In Unit 2 you have looked at the importance of considering lots of different viewpoints and different ways of studying. The most important trick for you will be to find a way of learning which works for you. Have a look at your first assignment and then have a go at answering the following questions.

1   Use the following table to check whether there are any areas of your studies that you feel particularly concerned about at the moment.

Table 14   How am I feeling about effective studying?

Study area	Better than I expected	OK so far	A bit confused	Really worried
Demonstrating understanding		✓		
Essay writing		✓		
Reading for study		✓		
Collecting and using evidence		✓		
Reflection		✓		
Evaluating ideas		✓		

2   Look at your grid and spend a few moments thinking about what you have learned. Write a short paragraph (about 150–200 words) telling your tutor about how your understanding or use of study skills has changed since you began the course. You do not need to find big changes – it may be a very small thing which you feel that you now have a clearer understanding of, or have had a chance to think about, or have gained more practice in.

COMMENT

I would expect most of your ticks to be in the middle two columns. If you have plenty of ticks in the first and second columns – well done! If you have more than you are happy with in the last two columns, then give your tutor a ring to talk through your concerns. Your tutor may be able to link you up with some helpful advice or support.

ESSAY

3 YOUNG PEOPLE FINDING THEIR PLACE

1 CHILDREN AND DECISIONS

CORE QUESTION
- How should children be involved in important decisions?

ROLES AND RESPONSIBILITIES

As Daisy has become older, she has had to think more about her role and responsibilities in the family, and has discussed this with her two best friends, Sammy and Sandeep. It is the children's last year in primary school, and their parents have already said that when they move schools they will be expected to take on more responsibility at home and also spend more time on school work. Having to think about and choose secondary schools led to much discussion in all the families about whether it is the children or the adults who choose, and who has the final say. There had been talk about Sammy and Sandeep going to private schools, which worried them all. They therefore had to think about their friendship, whether it would stand separation, and who they might have as friends in the future. They have attainment tests at school this term and know there will be pressure from the school to revise for them, and more homework than before. In addition to this, Daisy's mum Jodie, dad Graham and stepdad Eamon have talked with her about the need for her to take more responsibility in the home, which Daisy has resisted as she feels she is doing quite a lot already for someone her age.

Figure 38 Daisy, Sammy and Sandeep

Introduction for Essay?

1.1 HAVING A SAY AND BEING HEARD

Whatever age you are, you should be able to have a say in what you should be able to do, because it's as much your right as anyone else's.

(Child from the UK, in Thomas, 2001, p. 111)

Children do not necessarily have a say in important decisions in their lives. Adults may disagree about when children are old enough to have a say and also about the kinds of decisions which they should be involved in.

ACTIVITY 34	CHILDREN AS EXPERTS ON THEIR LIVES

Allow about 20 minutes

Read the following quotation by a German academic who lectures and researches in childhood studies. What do you think about this view?

Note down any reasons why you think that, according to the author, adults may be increasingly taking children's opinions into account. What reasons do you think adults may give for still being reluctant to involve children?

Essay para. Zinneker

> In the past when we wanted to learn something about the views and conditions of the young, we turned to their parents and teachers. Researchers, politicians, and educationalists were of the opinion that they were able to form more reliable judgements about children than the children themselves. This view is gradually crumbling; the authority of the adult in charge has become shaky. We are beginning to consider children as authorities who can speak for themselves. According to this new conviction it is they who know best how they are, what is good for them, and possibly even what is best for their own future and the future of their generation.

(Zinnecker, 2001, p. 45)

COMMENT

Did you think of any reasons why adults might increasingly feel that children should be involved in decision making? We thought that greater publicity of children's rights might be a factor, along with possible research showing that adults who had in the past spoken on behalf of children did not really represent children's views.

Essay para

We also felt, from our own experience as parents and from reading research, that there remains a reluctance to consult younger children. Age and therefore amount of life experience seem to remain important factors when allowing children to participate in decision making.

The media often like to portray children of this age as being out of control, causing problems or being problems, blaming parents for allowing them too much freedom. You may have experience of children aged 10 and 11 that challenges this. Children you know may take on responsibilities for shopping, caring for family members, choosing clothing, their schools, where their family lives and who they live with.

You may feel that it's OK for children to have a say and be listened to, but that doesn't necessarily mean they can have what they want, as adults do not always get what they want either. You may think that adults automatically know better because they have more life experience and have to take more responsibility for making a living, keeping the family life going and contributing to society in other ways.

Other reservations about children being in control might be about the principles or the practicalities. For example, you may think it depends on the age of the child, or whether they are disabled or not. You may think that some areas of children's lives are more worth consulting over than others – for example, small things like clothing, toys and food but not big things like where to go to school and where to live. There's also a difference between being consulted, and having the responsibility for the whole decision.

The above quotation by Zinnecker reflects a position that has become more widely accepted amongst researchers, politicians, policy makers and people who work directly with children in the UK and other Northern European countries.

The development and implementation of the United Nations Convention on the Rights of the Child and legislation such as the Human Rights Act 1998 has brought changes in the way children who use public services, such as schools, hospitals and social services, are treated. Adults who provide services to children and families are now expected to routinely consult with children, as you saw in Unit 2 in Cottesbrooke School's consultation with all pupils about the implementation of the Healthy Schools initiative. We also know that children and young people, including those with severe impairments, can communicate their views, and that even very young children can be supported to do so, as they were at Cottesbrooke.

Research studies show, however, that children are still not routinely asked their views or told by parents about things that affect them deeply. In one study of children in the West of England carried out by researcher Judy Dunn and her colleagues, a quarter of the children whose parents had separated said no one had talked to them about the separation when it happened (Dunn and Deater-Deckard, 2001). In another to do with money and living in a low-income family, most children said they were not told about family income or spending but, if they were, parents were more likely to discuss spending than income (Shropshire and Middleton, 1999). Children who cannot live with their parents also feel they are not consulted enough on decisions about their care:

> Basically the review meeting was about them – it was about what they thought was best for me … most of the time I don't need people to say what's best for me.

(Child in Thomas, 2001, p. 111)

Children and young people interviewed in surveys and studies have said strongly that they want to be consulted and listened to, and that their views and feelings should be seriously considered (Children and Young People's Unit, 2002; Brannen et al., 2000; Morrow, 1998). But this is not the same as expecting them to make the final decisions and to take responsibility for what happens as a

They need

? Use for Essay to discuss

result of them. Making final decisions is not necessarily what children in these studies said they wanted.

Help is available for adults who would like to involve children in decisions more actively but lack confidence in knowing how to go about it. In London the organization Coram Family has set up a national training, development and consultancy service called 'Listening to Young Children: A Participatory Approach', helping 'adults who want to improve their communication skills with children under the age of eight'; the organization has developed support resources (Lancaster, 2003). An organization called Triangle in Brighton, England, has particular expertise in communicating with disabled children, and offers training and consultancy for adults to do this as well (Triangle, 2003).

In this course unit, we are trying to directly represent children's views wherever possible, through their voices as they appear in research, through our compiled case study Family, and through children and parents we consulted while we were writing the course.

As authors and mothers of children aged 4, 6 and 12 at the time of writing, we agree with the messages in the quotations, and try to keep them in mind when bringing up our children. But this does not mean we put these beliefs into practice in rigid ways, for example, by always agreeing that our children know best. Parenting is about negotiation, and about recognizing the power adults have and children do not have. We believe that children's views should be sought as much as possible but that their more limited life experience has to be taken into account also. However, we do feel strongly that children should be able to make sense of why they may not have the final say in decisions.

1.2 PUTTING IT INTO PRACTICE

CHOOSING SCHOOLS

Daisy, Sandeep and Sammy had quite difficult discussions with their families about which school they should go to next. The school that was nearest to all of them, and in whose catchment area they lived, had not done that well in school inspections, and a new headteacher was due to be appointed for the coming school year. Daisy's family were split on where she should go. Graham was keen for her to be convent educated, and had offered to pay the fees. Jodie and Eamon wanted her to be able to walk, bus or cycle to school and felt the local high school was OK and that they would be able to support her if there were problems with school standards. Daisy wanted to go wherever Sammy and Sandeep went. Sandeep has cousins at a boy's private high school fifteen miles away, and the school also took boarders. Sandeep's dad and mum thought this could be useful for when his dad was away and his mum wasn't well, as his mum could go into short-break care if she wanted to. Sandeep wanted to be at school with his two friends, but loved his cousins and didn't mind the thought of being with them. Sammy's family all wanted her to go to the convent which was ten miles away but Sammy didn't want to go to school so far from home. She hated bus journeys and often felt travel-sick; and she had other friends apart from Daisy who would be moving to the local high school.

Effective study   Collecting and using evidence

When you are writing your essays you will be answering a question – the essay question. One of the important differences between a discussion with someone in the form of a conversation and an essay written for study is that your own opinion alone is not acceptable. You will be expected to find **evidence** to support, or prove, what you are describing or arguing. The good news is that evidence can come in many different forms – you have already looked at using observation and numerical charts or statistics to gather evidence. Most of the evidence that you will use in your essays, however, will be taken from the books that you are reading. This does not mean that you should copy large sections of each book into your essay. The trick is to be **selective** and find a short sentence or **quotation** which you think shows the reader what you are trying to explain. The next activity will give you a chance to practise finding neat quotations to support two different points.

ACTIVITY 35	WHAT SHOULD THE FAMILIES DO?

Allow about 15 minutes

You may want to re-read the last section of the case study, 'Choosing schools', now. Think about the big decision being made by the three families and select a quotation from the case study on:

- what each child wants to do
- the reasons why they may not be able to have their choice.

Table 15   Evidence of what each child wants, and reasons why they may not be able to have their choice

	What they want	Reasons against
Daisy		
Sammy		
Sandeep		

COMMENT

We have made some suggestions here – you may have picked out slightly different quotations. We could not find any evidence of why Sandeep should not do what he wanted as he was happy with either alternative.

Notice that the quotations are short, are copied exactly from the case study, are in inverted commas and are followed by a reference. A reference is the place where the original words were taken from; it is very important to show the reader that you are not pretending that these words are your own. You can also 'crop' your quotations, leaving out a bit at the beginning, end or even middle of the sentence if it is not relevant. If you do this, you will need to put dots (…) to show where you have left words out. Just make sure that you are confident that the sentence still makes sense when you edit it. If you feel unsure, it is better to put the whole sentence in rather than risk losing the meaning.

Table 16   What each child wants and why, continued

	What they want	**Reasons against**
Daisy	'Daisy wanted to go wherever Sammy and Sandeep went' (Y156 Unit 3, p. 119)	'Daisy's family were split on where she should go. Graham was keen for her to be convent educated, and had offered to pay the fees. Jodie and Eamon wanted her to be able to walk, bus or cycle to school and felt the local high school was OK and that they would be able to support her if there were problems with school standards.' (Y156 Unit 3, p. 119)
Sammy	'… Sammy didn't want to go to school so far from home. She hated bus journeys and often felt travel-sick' (Y156 Unit 3, p. 119)	'Sammy's family all wanted her to go to the convent which was 10 miles away …' (Y156 Unit 3, p. 119)
Sandeep	'Sandeep wanted to be at school with his two friends, but loved his cousins and didn't mind the thought of being with them.' (Y156 Unit 3, p. 119)	None

The likelihood of Sandeep getting his choice, as he is happy with either option, is high. Sammy's reasons are clear – to do with her physical health and comfort rather than the choice of school. Her family will need to take this seriously or she may not do well at school if she hates travelling. It's possible they could find car transport for Sammy and they may need to explore this. Once Sammy is decided, then Daisy's choice may be clearer – wherever Sammy goes. But if she chooses the convent, it presents other problems with distance and transport, and Jodie and Eamon being unhappy with the decision. The families are going to have to take more time to discuss the situation. What we also don't know are the different schools' admission policies and whether the children will have to compete for places. There is also the question of same-sex education for all of them, and going to a faith (Roman Catholic) school that will need to be discussed.

As you can see, it is not a simple question of what anyone wants. The implication of each choice has to be worked through with other members of the family, and some areas such as admission and selection criteria may be out of everyone's control. We discuss how it worked out for the children at the end of the unit.

We continue close to home in the next section by looking at children's views of their family life and working parents.

2   WHAT CHILDREN WANT FROM FAMILY LIFE AND WORK

CORE QUESTIONS

- What counts as a family?
- What do children think about working parents?

In this section we learn what children think about their families and family life, and what they expect from their working parents. We do this through research studies that feature children aged 10 and 11, through Daisy's views and those of her friends, and through the accounts of children and parents who were consulted while we developed this course. You will find that the children taking part in the research studies we feature, Daisy and her friends, and the children consulted for the course have very different lives, but that some common themes can be found about what they want from families. You will think about the implications of what the children say for parents and carers.

2.1 VIEWS ON FAMILY LIFE

'There isn't a right way to have a family ...' (Tara, in Brannen et al., 2000, p. 49)

Representations of what constitutes a 'proper family' are everywhere in the mass media and form powerful images in children's literature and in the minds and discourses of the adults who teach, care and take responsibility for children.

(Brannen *et al.*, 2000, p. 47)

The media image of a family is of a man and a woman, married, with a small number of children living together in their own home.

Most of us are born into some kind of family, although what and who counts as family is, despite the images presented in the media, very different for different people. Those who do not 'fit' the powerful media image can feel they count for less in the eyes of policy makers and service providers. Yet as we will see, children do not have rigid views of family life despite what the media say.

Effective study   Reflection

When studying subjects which are about 'people' and the way in which people interact with each other (such as those in health and social welfare and in education) you will often be asked to think about your own experiences. This is intended to add to your learning as you are likely to have relevant experience. Sometimes you will also be encouraged to draw upon such experiences when writing your essays.

It is important, however, that you are cautious about *when* and *how* you use your own experience as evidence in essays. Here are some points of caution to be aware of:

1   Not all academic subjects will accept personal experience. In fact many traditional subjects would criticize you for doing so. The subjects which are likely to welcome this kind of evidence are those which are closely related to learning to do a job (vocational subjects). *Understanding Children*, for example could lead you into studies preparing you to become a social worker, pre-school worker, teacher, psychologist, nurse etc. If you are unsure, check the guidance on writing essays on future courses or talk to your tutor.

2   Although your own experience can be used to give you insight into a subject and can be used to support a point that you want to make, it does not have the same status as evidence from published sources, such as books and research articles. Using your own experience may help the reader to understand the point you are making – much like we have tried to use pictures to illustrate this course book. This does not mean that your experiences prove that a point you are making is true for anyone apart from yourself, which is what research evidence tries to do. Let's look at an example.

Your views

What are your views on family life? What is a family to you, and what do you think families are for? Before moving to look at what children think, try the following activity.

ACTIVITY 36   YOUR VIEWS

Allow about 20 minutes

In this activity you will need to draw upon your own experiences. These could be your experiences of being in a family, as an adult or a child, or your observations of other people whom you know or even watch on TV. Using this experience, write down your answer to the following question:

•   Based upon your experience of the world, how would you define the word 'family'?

You can use as many words as you like.

COMMENT

There is no one answer to what a family is – you could say there are as many different kinds of family as there are families! The importance of using your experience is that it provides you with some evidence to contribute to the discussion. You have either observed or experienced a family and have an opinion about them. Some of the ideas of people we consulted for the course are given in the margin.

Who do you include as part of your family?

'Papa [this child's name for his father]; Carol [his aunt – mother's sister – who was visiting at the time]; Nana and Grandad [grandparents in Scotland]; Oma and Opa [grandparents in Germany] – what is the name of the aunt? [mother replies "Claudia"] Claudia; Jannika, Floriane, Fidelia [daughters of Claudia].'

'I think of a family as being a Mum, Dad and at least one child – pretty traditional really!'

'My partner and I aren't married and don't have kids – but I think we are still a family. Some people think we shouldn't have kids because we are both men, but I don't rule it out. I would like to foster at least.'

Did you have traditional views of a 'nuclear' family, or in other words married parents with their children? Or did you define family in its wider sense, to include several generations, same-gender couples and adults without children? You could also include children living in children's homes or even people living in communities such as communes or Jewish Kibbutzim.

While your own view as based on your own experience is 'true', it is not evidence of what all families are like. Without research to prove that your impression of a family is the same as everyone else's, or the only way in which a family could be understood, it remains your experience and quite weak evidence. Such research would then need to be scrutinized to test whether the findings and research were 'valid'. This is what academics mean by 'evidence'.

The changing nature of family life means that a smaller proportion of children than before live in what is called the traditional 'nuclear' family. Stepfamilies, lone-parent families and 'blended' families (where children and adults from different families combine and live together in new relationships) are more common than they were 40 years ago, as well as lesbian or gay households. There are differences between ethnic groups with South Asians and, particularly, Pakistani and Bangladeshi people more likely to be in married relationships with children than in other types of family (Modood *et al.*, 1997). Disabled children who use family-based short breaks may count their short break carer as part of the family. Grandparents and other relatives are increasingly being noticed by policy makers for their important role in family life and caring for children, as some communities have historically always done. Daisy's family and those of her friends are quite common examples of families today.

Children's views

We were interested to know what children's views were on the family. In order to do this we used information from two recent studies. One, by Julia Brannen and colleagues, included over nine hundred London girls and boys aged 10–12 from different ethnic groups. Through their schools, the children completed questionnaires. Some were interviewed on a one-to-one basis and others joined focus groups, where children come together with a facilitator to discuss questions in a structured way – a bit like the 'circle time' in schools where children have space to set their own agendas and discuss matters that concern them. The second study, by Virginia Morrow, was carried out in schools in two parts of East Anglia and involved one hundred and eighty-three children between the ages of 8 and 14, including a group of Pakistani children. These children drew and wrote their contributions, were asked to complete sentences in their own words, filled in a questionnaire and took part in group discussions.

ACTIVITY 37	CHILDREN'S VIEWS

Allow about 20 minutes

As you read what children had to say in the section below, compare their views with your own. Think about whether you agree with what the children thought families were for, and note down anything which surprises you or you find interesting about the children's views.

What counts as 'family'?

In both studies, children had a non-stereotyped and inclusive definition of families that reflected the families many of them were in. So, for example, lone-parent families and stepfamilies were included as well as those where there was a mother and a father present. In both studies, it was interesting that the presence of children was thought to make a family, and couples without children were therefore not counted as such. In the East Anglia study, some children of Pakistani background had one or both parents who were absent through visiting or working abroad, but they still were actively counted in as family. In many families from South Asia and the Caribbean, adult members including parents would live away from home for years but family ties would survive across the miles (see Olwig, 1993).

What do families 'do'?

A family is a group of people who love you. Families are for loving you and for being kind to you.

(James, 10, in Morrow, 1998, p. 25)

[Family] is the people you are related to and the people you care about.

[Families are] people who never ever don't care about you.

(Children, in Brannen *et al.*, 2000, pp. 47 and 205)

COMMENT

We were surprised that children were so clear that love was more important than the kind of blood ties or structures of families. Children seemed to us to be more accepting of the flexible and diverse nature of families and to have their priorities in absolutely the right place! While reflecting on their views we wonder about the debates which continue in governments about the acceptability of lesbian and gay people acting as foster and adoptive carers, and wonder if such adults in power are also able to be so clear about 'love' and 'dependability' being the most important aspect of a family.

These messages about families are powerful. It is hard to disagree with them, and the notion of unconditional love is a particularly powerful one. Of course, not all families offer this, but children seem very clear what they want, and what they have a right to expect.

In Virginia Morrow's study with East Anglian children, she found that they defined families in three ways. They defined them in terms of the **roles** they had and what members did for each other (for example, mother who makes the meals or father who does the shopping), the **relationships** (love and affection) and the **structure** (the people involved). Morrow found that the children used the term 'related to' to mean those they had relationships with, rather than in the narrow sense of blood relations.

Children in both studies strongly felt that the presence of love, care, mutual support, security and belonging were essential parts of their definitions of families. The relationships and what the families did for each other were therefore more important than what form the family took. In this way, they could have been making distinctions between 'good' and 'bad' families as far as they were concerned. Relationships are not always good ones though, and having a family doesn't mean you have good relationships. Some children who are in families would not have experiences like the children above, while some children living apart from their families may have.

Another area of family life that has constant attention is where parents work and their children need to be cared for. In the past, discussion used to be dominated by debate on whether or not mothers should work outside the home. You will see from the section below that children do not ask this question. Adults are not asking it as much as they did either.

2.2 WORKING PARENTS AND FAMILY LIFE

How do children feel about parents' work–life balance?

'Happy, because we can get money for the food we eat and the clothes we wear. Want Papa to spend less time at home so that he can get more money for us because we are quite poor. I want you [the mother] to spend more time at home because I love you.'

'My husband is unemployed and I work full-time. Our son does not have a good relationship with me and I feel that most of the time I spend with my son is spent policing his behaviour.'

In Julia Brannen and colleagues' research, children said that they would like parents to be 'there' for them, to not work too hard and to spend time with them.

| Effective study   Reading for study |

Reading actively can often involve more than just picking out relevant information for a particular purpose. You will often also have to think carefully about what you read and organize the information into different groups, or under different headings. This process can help you think critically about what the author is saying and whether you find what you are reading convincing.

Below is a summary of some of the findings from a study carried out in 1999 by Ellen Galinsky from the Families and Work Institute in New York. Galinsky presented these findings in London in April 2000. The study is based on interviews, focus groups and surveys sent to thousands of children and working parents throughout the USA. The children and families were chosen to reflect all the different groups in the population – different, for example, according to age, ethnicity and social class. This means that the researchers can be reasonably sure that the views are commonly held and not just those of, say, wealthy children or white children. The researchers asked parents and children for their views separately; their answers were then compared to see if parents' assumptions about what children want matched with what children had said. The author says she surveyed thousands of parents and children, but does not say how many replied so we do not know exactly how many she is talking about when she talks about percentages below.

Below, we look together at the children's views of their working parents and the messages they had for them.

ACTIVITY 38	ASK THE CHILDREN

Allow about 40 minutes

Read the article below. It contains some important messages about how children experience parents who work. After you have read it, use different colour pens to underline the points you already knew in one colour, found surprising in another and so on. Use the following headings:

1 Already knew
2 Surprising
3 Moving
4 Disturbing
5 Reassuring

Ask the children

What do children really think of working parents?

Contrary to what many parents think, the greatest wish children have is not to spend more time with parents or for them not to work. The biggest wish, given by 34% of the sample, was for parents to be less stressed when they are with them (only 21% of parents guessed this).

Kids play detective, listening to parents talk, sitting on the stairs, on the phone with mute button etc. in order to test what sort of mood parents are in. If trouble's in the air (and some reckon they can guess a parent's mood by the way they turn the front door handle as they get home) they have all sorts of techniques for avoiding a bad situation – jumping in the bath with the radio up high to drown out shouting, or even picking a fight in order to get the inevitable explosion over with.

Kids also spend a lot of time worrying about their parents when they are out or travelling, contrary to parents' notions of what their children thought of them. Children were asked to 'grade' parents according to internationally accepted standards of parenting skills. There was no difference in how working and non-working mothers were graded. Maternal employment was not the issue, values were: *how* we parent matters more than *what* we do. Disturbingly, 30% of children rated parents poorly on widely accepted parenting skills. [The authors did not say what these are.]

In the US, so much attention is still focused on the 'mommy war' (to work or not to work) that fathers tend to be overlooked. Yet in terms of time, it was fathers who children most wanted to spend time with. And as children grow older and become teenagers, they value time with parents more, paradoxically. Having more problems was one reason, regretting the breakdown in communication as they grew older and 'pushed parents away' was another.

In terms of childcare, the most happy arrangements tended to be where care was talked about in 'kith and kin' terms – i.e. 'she's like an auntie to us' – the new extended family? In addition to good childcare, having the support of family and friends around made the difference to how well mothers coped and were happy and productive at work.

So what needs to change?

Galinsky cited three areas for change:

1 **Change the debate** from whether mothers should or shouldn't work to how we as parents are when we're with our kids – do work pressures 'spill over' into time with the family, are fathers able to spend enough time with their children? We need to look at providing quality care and helping parents develop the support networks they need to 'navigate' work–life.

2 **Change the language** – children want more 'hang-around' time with parents when issues can emerge at their own pace, not to schedule. Parents need more 'focused time' which is not necessarily the same as quality time (which implies perfect family image) but time when they are not distracted by other issues and when problems can be aired along with other ups and downs of everyday life. Galinsky also favours the word 'navigate' to describe balancing work–life: this implies going with the flow, that you can't always predict the weather, some days rough, some calm yet having a sense of the direction you want to take.

3 **Change the behaviour** – having support in the workplace from parents helps, as does having some autonomy over how work gets done. How stressed work makes us is the real work–family variable, not whether we work or not.

Some surprises from the research

* 2 out of 5 children think their parents don't like their work – a lower rating than parents imagined.
* Children think we do better at work–life balance than we think we do.
* Children learn more about work from their mothers than their fathers.

The message from children

* Work if you want to work – kids will turn out the same either way.
* We are proud of you.
* Love us, raise us well, even when we are difficult.
* Discipline but don't be harsh or judgemental.
* Keep your promises.
* Keep on working and supporting your children.
* Spend focus and hang-around time with us – the more time you spend, the better.
* Put your family first.
* Be there for your children – *or else*.
* Take care of your kids – one day they may take care of you.
* Don't take stresses at work into the home.
* Find out what's going on in your kid's lives (only 35% of kids rated their parents an 'A' for knowing).
* Talk to your kids even if they act like they don't want you to.
* Teach your children how to work and do something they enjoy.

   (Daniels and McCarraher, no date, 'Ask the children' (online), http://www.radlogic.demon.co.uk/page23.html to page25.html)

COMMENT

Did you manage to find something to put under each heading? It could be that you already knew all of the content of this research – although this would be surprising. You should still, however, be able to organize the information here into the last three categories.

* When we read this article we were expecting that, more than anything, the children in the survey wanted their parents to be able to cut off from work when they were home, and not to take their work problems out on them. They wanted parents to be 'there' for them, to find out what is important in their children's lives and to talk to them. In summary, they seemed to want good quality relationships with their parents.

* We were surprised and pleased, however, that they took it for granted that mothers worked outside the home. Children also worried about their parents when they were away, which challenges the idea that they usually only think about themselves.

* As authors, we found reading this article really moving, and it made us think hard about how much we take our work home 'emotionally' and let it 'spill over' into family life. Working from home as we are able to do

doesn't help the situation either as there has to be a conscious effort to separate from one and focus on the other. We were also moved that children wanted to spend more time with their fathers.

- But we were disturbed by what the children said about wanting their parents to be less stressed, and how many of them rated their parents poorly in their parenting skills. Neither children nor parents can enjoy life properly feeling like this.

MAKING CHANGES AT HOME

After a particularly bad week when her father, grandmother, aunt and uncle had all been very busy and stressed at work (they all work in the family food take-away business), Sammy was feeling 'got at'. Nothing she had done seemed to be right and she had been criticized for not helping out enough, which she felt was unfair. She knew the stress wasn't because of anything she had done, but she nevertheless felt a bit low. Back at Sandeep's house, Sammy, Daisy and Sandeep talked about parents and work and how their parents and other family members had problems 'switching off', and sometimes took their feelings out on the children. They wondered if other children felt like this too. They searched the internet for 'working parents' and came across the article you have just read, which they printed off. It is a bit different for Sammy as they live above the take-away business; this means dad and other family members go downstairs to work, rather than going 'out'. Because of this, work and home were not separate. Jodie also worked from home at times and this had caused problems in the past as well. The children nevertheless decided to show the article to their parents and use it to get a discussion going that evening about how they feel.

Once Daisy got home, she asked if she could talk to Eamon and Jodie before she went to bed. It's always hectic at bedtimes with Eamon's shift work, Ryan's reluctance to go to sleep and Mia staying awake for as long as she needs to. Mealtimes are also busy so Daisy tries to grab what time she can. She gave Jodie and Eamon a copy of the article and asked them to read it and come and talk to her before she fell asleep. They seemed reluctant, saying they hadn't time to read anything, but she pleaded and they saw it was important to her.

Reading the article made a difference to Jodie and Eamon. They realized they gave what little spare time they had to Mia and Ryan and that, because Daisy is older, she was taken for granted and may not have been getting the attention she deserves. Eamon was also aware of his stepparent relationship with Daisy and how he can't 'be there' for her in the same way Graham can. They went to see Daisy and asked her if they could all think about what to do and to have another talk the next day. Daisy sent a phone text-message to her friends suggesting they met after school.

At the children's meeting the next day, they shared their experiences. All the family members had listened and read the article. Sammy's grandmother had cried, Sandeep's mother too, but that had been OK. Sandeep's dad had suggested they draw up a 'working parent's agreement' rather like the kind of things Daisy's parents sometimes did when they felt she hadn't been helping round the home enough.

Figure 39 We don't like it when you behave in stressy ways.

This is what they wrote:

WORKING PARENTS AGREEMENT BETWEEN XXX AND XXX

We do not like it when you behave in stressy ways and take it out on us if you have had a bad day.

We feel it is unfair when we are picked on and if we are the oldest we get it more.

When mums work we see more of them than we do when our dads work. We want to spend more time with dads. Sammy's dad is like a mum but she still doesn't see him enough.

We want time that is our time with you. We know it is hard but can we try?

We want to tell you about the things we do but you don't ask us.

SO

Tell us if you have a bad day and say it is not our fault. Say sorry.

Don't be mean just to make you feel better.

Let us see our dads more or talk to them more.

Talk to us more about what we are doing.

Give us non-stressy time together.

Sammy wants to be a bit freer to do things with us.

When Sandeep's mum is not well, can we all go round to his place so we can see him a bit more?

How it all worked out

Sammy managed to negotiate two evenings off a week when she did not need to help out in the take-away business. Her father, aunt and uncle and her grandmother were a bit taken aback and disapproved of her discussing the family with her friends, but did listen in the end. Sandeep's mother and father and uncle were sorry but felt they had little choice over how they worked, though they did agree to spend family time together on a Friday evening every week if they could. Daisy got a promise that as soon as Ryan was more settled at school, she would have an evening or part of a weekend that was 'her time' to spend with her mum and Eamon if she wanted, in whatever way she liked. They also decided to involve Graham in the discussion, though he did manage to give quality time to the children when he saw them, and was not easily stressed.

2.3 COMMUNICATION AND CONSULTATION ABOUT FAMILY LIFE

Essay

In the example above the young people were able to take hold of something that was worrying them and discuss it with their families. Perhaps they were lucky in that they felt the adults would at least listen to them for long enough so they could raise the issue. Not all children can trust their parents to do this.

Studies have found that children can understand the complexities of family life and expect to have to negotiate their position in decisions. The fact that children have strong and clear feelings about what they want is an excellent reason for involving them in decisions. Children who can't express these feelings can be helped to communicate in a range of ways. What is not acceptable, is to ignore the children or what they have to tell us.

As well as finding out what children think about family life and working parents, another area receiving attention is how children contribute to family life. We look at this in the next section.

Key points

- Children need to be given the opportunity to participate in making important decisions which affect their lives.

- Families take many forms; the important common factor for children is love and dependability.

- Children accept working parents as a normal part of life, but want their needs recognized by busy and stressed adults.

3   CHILDREN'S CONTRIBUTIONS TO FAMILY LIFE

CORE QUESTION

• What part do children play in family life and the family economy?

In this section we look at the range of ways children aged 10 and 11 help in the home and contribute to the family economy. We do this through children's experiences as told in research studies, and those of Daisy and her friends from our case-study family. We feature a girl and a boy from Chittagong, Bangladesh, and consider the similarities and differences between their experiences and those of children in the UK. We also identify skills that children of this age can develop through being actively involved in this way.

Figure 40 Daisy, Sandeep and Sammy doing things for the family.

3.1 CHILDREN DO MORE THAN ADULTS THINK

Some adults in the UK may think children of this age are a drain on resources in a family. But there is evidence now from the UK and elsewhere in Europe of how much children of this age *contribute* to the family economy and to family life. This does not necessarily mean income they earn from paid work (as the age of employment is generally regulated by law), although paid work is also relevant.

By *contributions*, we mean children's role in keeping a home going in other ways, for example, through emotional support and chores around the home. We also consider the skills children learn from this work, and those they gain that their parents may not have, for example, in using new technologies. You will read about research that highlights children's contributions that are often hidden. You will also find out what part Daisy and her friends play in their families and how you can be more aware of these children's essential roles in family life.

When you were a child, your parents may have treated childhood as a preparation for being an adult, making sure you learned to do the practical things you would need to be able to survive when you grew up. Or they may have taken the view that childhood was a time when children should be free of responsibility for as long as possible and should not be troubled with adult-type tasks. It may be that your parents did not give out such clear messages at all, or you had a mixture of responsibility and 'freedom'. How much choice you or your family had over these matters would also depend on family finance, family values and expectations. If money is short, cleaning the car saves a fee; if the family is large, it is unreasonable to expect one person to do all the cooking and cleaning. The next section gives you a chance to think about this through the experiences of Daisy and her friends.

HELPING OUT IN FAMILY LIFE

Daisy and her friends are typical of the ten-year-olds in their school. Their families have enough money but can't buy luxuries or large items or have a family holiday without a struggle. Daisy and her friends are expected to take some responsibility in the home and help out in other ways too. Below we look at the kinds of contributions they are making in their families.

We asked Daisy, Sandeep and Sammy to tell us what they did to help out in family life. Read what they had to say:

Daisy:

> On the days she goes to my grandparents I get Mia up and dressed, and feed our cat called Paws before I go to school. When Eamon comes in from work he takes Mia to Grandma and Grandpa. If I get back before anyone else after school I get the tea ready, check the phone messages and write them down. I then do my homework, or do

it later while Mia is getting ready for bed. At the weekend, if I clean the car or do some of the laundry I get a pound. Sometimes on Saturday if Grandpa needs me to help with his wheelchair I go with him shopping. One of my favourite jobs is selling all the stuff we don't want at a car boot sale every month. I go with my Dad and Rosalind and we have a great time.

Sandeep:

When Mum is not well she can't go to work and can't do hardly anything in the home. When Dad's away Uncle Raj helps out but he works long hours and my school is close by so I come home at lunchtime to see she's OK and we have lunch together. I'm good at making quick snacks. When Mum's ill I do some of the housework and Uncle does the cooking in the evening. My sister is doing her GCSEs so we give her time to study but she helps when she can. When Dad is home and Mum is ill I don't do very much. They say I should have time to be a child as well. When Mum is well, she has lots of energy and does nearly everything! Oh, I also do a paper round on Thursdays and Sundays with my cousin who is 15. It's his job and we do it after school or on Sunday morning but he pays me half as we get it done in half the time.

Sammy:

I live with my dad and my grandmother, aunt and uncle. We have a take-away food shop. When I was little I didn't have to do very much to help out, but now I am older it's expected. I don't always mind, but I do mind in the summer when I could be out playing. Dad knows this and sometimes will give me some money to make up for what I am missing. And I get more time off in the summer. I do like being by the counter though to say hello to people and give the orders to my aunt who is the cook when Nanna has taken them. I know lots of people – they say hello to me on the street. I often go to the cash-and-carry with Dad and really enjoy choosing all the different food, and to the vegetable market with my aunt.

ACTIVITY 39	VALID AND VALUABLE

Allow about 30 minutes

Now read the accounts again and, using a highlighter pen, mark all the different ways the three children say they contribute to the household – for example, going to the vegetable market, cleaning the car, doing a paper round. Then list these under the categories below, marking with a tick what each child does.

Table 17 The way children contribute

Type of contribution	Daisy	Sandeep	Sammy
Housework	✓	✓	
Meal preparation or cooking	✓	✓	
Shopping	✓		✓
Child care/companionship	✓		✓
Help in family business	✓	✓	✓
Adult care		✓	
Pet care			✓
Selling things	✓	✓	✓
Other (paper round, babysitting, phone messages)	✓	✓	

COMMENT

You will see from your chart just how much each child does to help in the home. Some of these jobs are mainly practical; others give emotional support to family members. Daisy takes quite a bit of responsibility for Mia and also for doing other set tasks in the home. For example, she cares for their pet cat, assists Michael when shopping, takes down phone messages. She can earn money from small jobs at the weekend. Sandeep gives his mother emotional and practical help when she is ill, making meals and coming home from school to see that's she's OK. He also earns money through helping with a paper round. Sammy's helping out in the business is a big contribution, and she takes on a variety of different jobs such as greeting customers, taking messages and shopping. Far from being a drain on resources, these children's contributions are essential to the smooth running of their families' lives. They add to their families just by being part of them.

Research studies on children's contributions

In Julia Brannen and colleagues' study with London children the researchers used an imaginary situation to get at children's views. They asked about a 12-year-old South Asian girl whose parents owned a shop which was open till 9 p.m. When she comes home from school, and has homework to do, should she help her parents in the shop? The majority of children said she should, but were clear that it should not be for very long and that she should be able to do her homework. The South Asian children in the research did not stand out as having different views from the other children. In this respect, Sammy's situation is similar; she is expected to help out in the family take-away business and accepts this as part of her own life rather than just that of the adults in her family. A researcher called Miri Song (1999) has interviewed and written about Chinese young people's work in family take-away businesses, and how much this was an accepted part of their family life, rather than being seen as an imposition. In this type of work there is overlap between what

*Research helps
to build a case
for change and
to build on
what is your
Practice!*

Julie Brennan

adults do and what children do, and children also come to understand what parents' world of work is like, instead of it being separate and invisible. But what the children in Brannen and colleagues' study are reminding us, is that children have other responsibilities to fulfil, such as being a schoolchild, and that parents should not expect too much from them.

Brannen's research is an example of the way in which researchers try to collect evidence about a subject using a method that will convince other people interested in the subject that their results or findings are 'true'. One method of trying to get evidence that is more reliable than one person's opinion (such as your own experience) is to ask lots of people the same question. This is what Julia Brannen and her researchers did.

ACTIVITY 40	HELPING OUT AT HOME

Allow about 20 minutes

Julia Brannen and her colleagues used a questionnaire (or a set of written questions) to ask children about:

1 Any help with housework they gave at home
2 What they did
3 Why they did it.

Have a look at the table below which shows how much housework they said that they did.

Table 18 Housework done			
Amount of housework	A lot	Some/a little	None at all
Percentage of children	32	65	3

Only a small percentage of children said they did not help at all, about a third said they did 'a lot' of housework and the rest did 'some or a little'.

The researchers also divided the work into 'self-care' tasks and 'family-care' tasks, as shown in the next table, and asked the children to identify which ones they had done in the past week.

Now have a look at the next table.

1 Note down what were the most common tasks under each heading (self-care and family-care).

2 Try to note down some of the information you would like to know that this table does *not* tell you.

Table 19 Type of housework

Self-care tasks	Every day (%)	Some days (%)	Not at all (%)	Total number of children
Making something to eat for yourself	37	55	8	802
Clear away own dirty dishes	31	46	23	799
Tidy/clean own room	28	56	16	811
Wash own sports kit	8	24	68	799
Family-care tasks	**Every day (%)**	**Some days (%)**	**Not at all (%)**	**Number**
Lay/clear table	26	49	25	797
Wash up/fill or empty dishwasher	21	43	36	791
Make something to eat for someone else	18	60	22	803
Vacuum or dust	16	57	27	800

Source: Brannen *et al.*, 2000, p. 159

COMMENT

1 The most common self-care tasks were tidying their own room, making something to eat for themselves, clearing away their own dirty dishes and washing their own sports kit. Family-care tasks were laying and clearing tables, washing up or filling/emptying the dishwasher, making something to eat for someone else and vacuuming or dusting.

2 There are lots of things that this table does not tell us. This may be because the information is not included in this particular table, or it could be because the information was not included in the questionnaire. In fact if you read the research in full you would find that it does include the information about what the children enjoyed, differences between girls and boys, and reasons for helping.

Over half the children said they enjoyed helping, but the girls were more likely to say this than the boys. Other reasons given were to be helpful to parents, because everyone in the family helps each other, they were told to help, they got paid to help and, for some, it was a clear preparation for independence.

REASONS FOR HELPING

We asked Daisy, Sandeep and Sammy their reasons for helping.

Daisy:

> Because there is a lot to do and Mum and Eamon can't do it all and also I enjoy going out with Grandpa and I can earn pocket money for some of the jobs I do.

Sandeep:

> Well, I couldn't leave Mum alone when she is not well. The paper round is great fun and I have learned how to do the easy cooking which will be good for me when I grow older.

Sammy:

> It's expected – everyone helps in our family. I like lots of the things I do, but not so much in the summer when I want to be with my friends. But it's better now.

How much children are expected to help in the home will depend on a number of things – for example, the parents' views on childhood; their view on child's work and adult's work; how many people live in the home and whether the parent is alone or living with another adult.

3.2 CARING TASKS AND EMOTIONAL SUPPORT

Julia Brannen and her colleagues asked children what they did that counted as general caring tasks. The results are listed in the table below.

Table 20 Children's contribution to general caring by frequency

	Every day (%)	Some days (%)	Not at all (%)	Total number of children
Help mother / stepmother / female foster carer	50	47	3	820
Be nice to / help classmates	37	57	6	818
Look after pets	37	21	42	800
Help father / stepfather / male foster carer	36	48	16	800
Be nice to brothers / sisters	26	62	12	815
Take care of younger brothers / sisters	25	30	45	775
Help an elderly person	16	56	28	815

Source: Brannen *et al.*, 2000, p. 162

These results showed some differences in replies according to ethnic group. South Asian children were more likely to live in two-parent households, and were more likely to report helping their fathers than children from other ethnic groups. South Asian children who were the oldest or middle children in a family were also more likely to report caring for younger sisters and brothers every day than other groups. They also, together with black children (those of African and Caribbean backgrounds), were more likely to report being nice to brothers and sisters every day, compared to other groups of children.

Our case-study children contributed to caring tasks in a number of ways too. Daisy cared for Mia and their pet cat most days, and supported her grandfather when he needed it; Sandeep cared for his mum when she wasn't well and all of them could be said to be giving general help to their fathers and their mothers if they were there.

An area where children's contribution has often not been acknowledged by parents, policy makers and the general public is where children take on caring responsibilities for adults. This can be looking after a parent or other family member who is physically or mentally ill, or who may be disabled. Sometimes these children are pitied, as if they are 'burdened' with caring, and for some children it can feel like this if they do not get support from outside services or other family members. However, in some families, just as Sammy is content to help out in the take-away, children also take responsibility for care if their parents or other relatives need them to, and do not see it as a 'burden' (see research by Adele Jones and colleagues, 2002). This was the case for Sandeep when his mother had episodes of illness and also for Daisy who helped her grandfather.

It can be hard for children in these caring roles though. Sometimes they are not able to discuss their role with anyone and lack support. They may not define themselves as a 'young carer' and so not want to join a group of this name. Schools and the general public can see what they are doing as a 'problem' that interferes with their school and childhood, rather than being part of their life that needs accommodating. More awareness of what support these children want is needed.

In addition, Brannen's research found that many children provided comfort and a listening ear, particularly for their mothers. This is reassuring to read, particularly as it challenges the common image of children as selfish and uncaring and even 'demons' as often portrayed by the media (Goldson, 2001).

3.3 LOOKING FURTHER AFIELD

In Europe and the United States of America, research is also focusing more on children's contributions to family life. This research tends to be carried out amongst the more affluent countries in the northern hemisphere (such as America and Europe), where children's lives can be very separate from adults – they spend a lot of time with other children at school and outside school. In countries such as Bangladesh children in wealthy families share a lot with these northern children as video-cassette film from another Open University course has shown (OU, 2002, Video 2), but the expectations on the majority of others can be very different. They are needed to keep the family going and their paid and unpaid labour is essential. In the video and associated activity below, we ask you to compare the daily lives of two children who live in Chittagong in Bangladesh with those of Daisy, Sandeep and Sammy in the UK. The children are Bilkis, a girl aged about 11 who lives in the city, and Tinco, a boy aged about 12 who lives in a village.

Effective study   Developing and demonstrating understanding

A key part of developing understanding is to organize information in a meaningful way. This is very important when you write your essays. During your studies you will need to use ideas and information from different places, or sources. Some of the information and ideas will be directly from what you have read, but some may be from video or audio recordings. As you move through your studies in the future you will come across many different kinds of written information, such as articles from published books or research, statistics or diagrams. To demonstrate that you have understood a subject well enough to answer an essay or examination question, you will need to select and organize information from different sources in a thoughtful and reasoned way.

In order to demonstrate that you have thought logically about the selection and organization of your chosen sources, you will also need to explain why you have selected them. The next activity will give you an opportunity to practice selecting and organizing information and also commenting on why you have included it.

ACTIVITY 41   CHILDREN'S LABOUR: ESSENTIAL WORK

Allow about 45 minutes

DVD Band 6

Watch DVD Band 6. It shows Bilkis's and Tinco's daily lives. For this activity we want you to focus on the work they do that contributes to their households. As you watch, think about the type of contribution to the family that each child makes.

Figure 41   Tinco and Bilkis

Watch the video extract through again, this time using the table below to write down how each child spends their day. We have used the same table you used for Daisy and her friends. Put a tick in the relevant boxes.

Also use the numbers 1–3 to indicate whether they spend a lot (3), some (2) or just a little (1) time on each activity.

Table 21 Types of contributions

	Tinco		Bilkis	
	Tick	1, 2 or 3	Tick	1, 2 or 3
Housework		2	✓	
Meal preparation or cooking			✓	3
Shopping	✓	2	✓	
Child care		1		
Help in family business	✓	3	✓	2
Adult care		1		
Pet care		1	✓	
Selling things	✓	3		
Other work (paper round, babysitting, fishing, housework for someone else)				3

Now look at the lists you made for the children in England in Activity 39, and compare them with the ones for the children in Bangladesh. Write a few lines about the similarities and differences you found. Did the England checklist cover all the things the children did in Bangladesh, and vice versa?

COMMENT

Did you notice how the paid work Tinco did or the housework Bilkis carried out for her landlady was essential for the economic well-being of their families? Even though Tinco says it is up to him whether he fishes or plays, at other times he says his money pays for their daily needs. Sammy's labour is important too, as the family might have to employ someone else, or work that bit harder if she wasn't around. But she does not have to go away from home to do the work. Sandeep's paper round earns him money that otherwise his parents would have to pay. However, this kind of paid work takes up more of the Bangladeshi children's time than it does for UK children.

There is also a sense of responsibility felt by Tinco and Bilkis that may be different for many UK children. Tinco says that when he is older and his older brother leaves home, he will take responsibility for his whole family, including his parents. Bilkis is clear that she has to go to work at her landlady's even when her mother is ill and can't work there as well. So although there are gender differences in the kind of work they are expected to do now, the notion of responsibility is clearly set at their age.

In countries such as Bangladesh, there is debate going on about whether children should be involved in paid work. There are many arguments for and against. Arguments 'for' include the essential contribution to the family who might otherwise be extremely poor, the development of skills as it is real work, and the self-esteem it brings. Arguments 'against' include the exploitation, poor pay and dangerous working conditions experienced; their rights as a child to be able to play and study; work can interfere with children's development and schooling. However, Martin Woodhead (2003), a researcher at the Open University, was involved in a study of children aged 10–14 years. Three hundred children in Bangladesh, Ethiopia, the Philippines and Central American countries were asked if what was best for them was only going to work, only going to school, or doing both. Over three-quarters of them opted for both working and going to school. It may be difficult here to separate out the children's views from what is expected of them by their families and cultures, or what they take to be the realities of their lives. But we cannot ignore the strength of feeling expressed by these children, and general policies to abolish child labour will not necessarily help them or their families.

3.4 WHAT SKILLS ARE CHILDREN LEARNING?

Far from being 'takers' of family life, we have seen that children across the world are essential contributors, and that this happens in the UK as well. But children are also learning life skills, which adults may not realize or give them credit for.

ACTIVITY 42   **LIFESKILLS AUDIT**

Allow about 30 minutes

Look back at the tables you filled in for the five children in Activities 39 and 41. For each of the areas mentioned, think about and write down the skills the children are learning or developing when they are involved in household and family tasks or contributing to them.

You can list them under these categories:

- Practical skills
- Communication and intellectual skills
- Emotional skills
- Self-help skills
- Business skills.

COMMENT

We noted the following for Bilkis:

- Practical skills: cleaning, laundry
- Communication and intellectual skills: playing with landlord's child; negotiating tasks to do; retaining a schedule
- Emotional skills: managing relationships outside the home

- Self-help skills: getting somewhere on time; completing a task without supervision; taking responsibility
- Business skills: managing workload, juggling priorities.

All the children are developing some skills from each category that will help them get on in their lives. Far from spending all their time at school or in play, the children we are featuring show themselves to be quite responsible.

We hope that through reading the children's accounts and watching the video extracts of their lives you have seen just how much they contribute to their families, and how much they are valued and valuable members of society. There were differences in how each of the children contributed to the family and family income, but they all did in some way, and through these activities developed a range of skills. We hope that these insights have helped to counteract the negative images of children of this age that are sometimes portrayed in the media and elsewhere.

4   CHILDREN AND FRIENDSHIPS

CORE QUESTION

• What is important about children's friendships?

In the next section, we look at another important aspect of life for children aged 10 and 11 – friendships.

FRIENDSHIPS

Handwritten margin notes: ← Sage

Children need to build the confidence + "learn to move on" "we learn to move on" Daisy, Sammy + Sandeep

Daisy, Sandeep and Sammy have been friends since they began school and sat at the same table to work in class. Having to choose new schools brings the possibility that they might not be together so much in the future. This made them think a lot about friendships. Daisy recalls:

> When we were talking about where we would like to go to school next year, I thought that the most important thing was that we should all be together. Sammy and Sandeep agreed that it was important, but that other things were important too. Sammy said she could not go to a school her family were unhappy with; Sandeep agreed and said that being with his cousins was also important to him. He had visited their school and liked it a lot. I was upset. I kind of thought we would just go through school together. Sammy and Sandeep said we would all stay friends even if we went to different schools, but I think it will be hard.

Daisy was quite convinced that she would not have any friends if she had to leave Sammy and Sandeep. They decided to see if this was really true. They asked Daisy to make a list of her close friends at school, and those who were not as close. She also made a list of the places she went and people she saw when she was not at school, and not with Sammy and Sandeep.

Daisy's list of friends at school:

• Close friends: Sammy, Sandeep

• Other friends: Oliso, Rachel, Priya, Loren, Jessica

• Places I go out of school: Dad's friend's house; swimming with Dad; theatre group on Wednesdays; shopping with Grandpa

• Who I see there: Simone (Dad's friend's daughter); Loren (theatre group); Gemma (theatre group); Jane (Grandpa's neighbour's daughter)

Making a list of what Daisy actually did and who she saw was useful for her. Although she cared about Sammy and Sandeep most of all, when she talked about the children on her list of 'other' friends, she could imagine being better friends with some of them. This didn't feel quite so bad. She then thought about the three girls she saw regularly who were not at her school. It had been easy to make friends with them. Perhaps she *might* be able to survive without Sammy and Sandeep after all.

[handwritten margin notes: Julia Brennan. The quality of friendship was more important than the number of friends]

4.1 HAVING FRIENDS

[handwritten: Tutorial Lg.]

Of course, not every child will share Daisy's, Sammy's and Sandeep's experiences. For some children, friendships will be much more difficult to make and keep. Julia Brannen and her colleagues asked the children in their study to list the friends they had, and how important they were to them. They concluded that the actual number of friends children had was less relevant to them than the *quality* of their friendships. But even so, they found that children in foster care had fewer friends than other children, which they linked to research evidence of fostered children needing to use their emotional energy to build relationships with foster carers and their families, and to keep up contact with their own families. This, plus the likelihood of them having to leave friends behind when moving in foster care, could explain their lack of friends. Some of the fostered children in her study did emphasize the importance of having friends. However, fostered children were not always as free to bring their friends home as some of the other children. Children can also experience other barriers to friendship, which we will look at later in the section.

> **How do you choose your friends?**
>
> 'People who are nice to me — and the others give me Chinese burns.'
>
> 'My friends keep me company and make me happy and give me happy dreams.'
>
> (8-year-old boy)

The Brannen research distinguished between 'having friends' which looked at the numbers and importance of friends in their lives, with 'being friends' which looked at details of the actual relationships.

4.2 BEING FRIENDS

What's important about friends? We asked Kiran, the (at the time) 11-year-old daughter of one of the course authors, to give us her views:

> Everyone needs friends because they need someone to turn to and they need people who are the same as them. It is important to be able to trust a friend. You have to choose someone who you can be yourself around. It's useless to have a friend if you just put on an act around them. If you are true friends, you'll never get bored with each other!

[handwritten margin notes: I agree. Family versus Friends]

The children in the Brannen study echoed her views. Friends were 'there for you' and could provide a great deal of support. There were some who rated them as important as family, with many finding friends an alternative source of support to family in some respects. This was when there were things they couldn't talk to family about. South Asian children, though, were more likely to say that family was more important than white or black (African background) children.

In searching for video material to illustrate children's friendships at this age, we again feature Bilkis who you met earlier in this unit. We follow Bilkis and her friends after they finish school one day.

| **ACTIVITY 43** | **BEING FRIENDS IN BANGLADESH** |

Allow about 30 minutes

DVD Band 7

Watch DVD Band 7. As you watch, think about the relationships Bilkis and her friends have, and how you can tell from the video that they are close friends. You may need to watch the extract more than once.

Make notes on what Bilkis says about the things she values about friendship.

We will return to the video in the next activity.

COMMENT

Although the friendship is very much told from Bilkis's point of view, it is clear that the girls enjoy being together and sharing the games, food preparation and eating. Bilkis acknowledges that there can be tensions and jealousies between them – for example, by Taslema having lots of other friends and wanting to spend time with them as well. But she firmly believes that arguments with 'lifelong friends' should be sorted out in the end.

Bilkis values the notion of 'lifelong friends' and talks a lot about the friendship bond. It is clear that she and her two friends have much in common – they all work for other people in the mornings and then attend school in the afternoons. She talks about them being 'good girls' which she uses to distinguish themselves from boys (who she sees as bad) but also from 'local girls' – who live in Bilkis's locality but presumably don't attend school. One of the things she specifically mentions is how Taslema and Kobita defended her against 'local girls' when she was in an argument.

The concept of friends being 'forever' is a powerful one.

Kiran, in the quotation on the previous page, talks about shared interests, true friends never being bored with each other, trust and being able to 'be yourself' with friends.

4.3 WHAT FRIENDS DO TOGETHER

It is common to think that children of this age have little more than a home life and a school life. At school, children's free time with friends is limited to break times and lunchtime. Families will also differ enormously as to whether they encourage children to bring friends home. For some, there is just no room in the home for anyone else; for others, home is a place for family only. Other families may have an 'open-door' policy where anyone is welcomed as friends, and yet other families will closely control the friendships their daughters and sons have. However, the leisure and non-school lives children have with friends have had little attention and we are only just getting to know about them. It can sometimes seem that children's lives are so governed by rules about where they can and can't play, and what they can and can't do, and who with, that they don't have time to just 'hang about' together. We shall see if this is true for the children we have met in this course unit so far.

Effective study Evaluating ideas

When you evaluate ideas in your studies you are bringing together all of the areas of effective study that we have been talking about in *Understanding Children*. You need to read and understand different people's views and you need to collect and make sense of evidence. In addition to this you need to be able to build your argument and draw your own conclusions. Having thought carefully about the evidence and different people's ideas, what do *you* think? What is your 'position' or point of view about a subject, based on the ideas and evidence that you have looked at?

Read again ///

ACTIVITY 44

WHAT BILKIS LOVES TO DO

Allow about 20 minutes

DVD Band 7

Watch DVD Band 7 again. This time you will need to observe and think about:

1 what Bilkis and her friends get pleasure in doing together
2 what is interesting or unusual about this example of Bilkis playing with her friends.

This task then requires you to pick out any differences between Bilkis's life and the lives of children that you are familiar with, or perhaps your expectations of children living in Bangladesh.

COMMENT

1 Bilkis and her friends play games such as skipping and Kut-Kut, and sing and dance together. They also buy, prepare and eat food together.

2 We were struck by how simple the things they do are, yet how much pleasure they can give. Buying ingredients – cucumber and tamarind – for making a favourite dish, preparing it together and then eating it together from the same dish, seems such an obvious way to cooperate and share an activity. It's healthy too, rather than the diet of sweets and crisps preferred by many UK children. Yet this kind of activity is one that the UK children of this age we know certainly don't do spontaneously, and would usually involve adult supervision.

Study note

In this last activity you have begun to go beyond the first stage of essay writing, which is reproducing or describing what you have read or viewed. The ideas that you thought of for question 2 were not stated in the video, but you came up with them by thinking about what you saw and comparing this with your own previous knowledge. You have taken in new information, thought about it in the context of what you already know and provided some original ideas of your own based upon your thoughts. This is an important step towards thinking and writing for study.

By way of contrast, we asked Kiran, also then aged 11, to write down how she spent two hours after school one day in May 2003 when she went home with her friend.

> First, when we had walked back to her place, I went to her room while she practised her cello. She then let me have a go and I taught her how to play some tunes on a keyboard, and we had a right laugh. Then we did 'Stars in their Eyes' and a few drama sketches, then we went off to our drama group.

Notice how the two of them have access to musical instruments, and that their games are influenced by television programmes. They too attend school together and share the same interests such as music and drama. They were well able to make up their own entertainment and games that they played together in the same way as Bilkis and her friends did.

Children in the UK have more access to prepared food to eat, to items like videos, computer games and television to help them fill their time. They can also be under surveillance more: with many parents anxious by reports of child abduction and murder, they are not always allowed to spend time away from home together without parents knowing where they are. Mobile phones have made it much easier for children to be away from home and keep in touch though, and many children of this age in the UK have their own phone, even if parents are not that well off.

On the other hand, there may be differences in what is permitted for boys and girls, with boys more likely to be allowed to play away from home at an earlier age.

4.4 THE IMPORTANCE OF 'JUST HANGING OUT'

TIME WITH FRIENDS

Daisy, Sammy and Sandeep made a list of the things they did when they were together over a period of a week. This is what it looked like:

Table 22   Daisy's, Sammy's and Sandeep's week

Mon	Walk to school the long way, find bird's nest with no eggs in
	At lunchtime, cross-country running club
	After school, at 3:30 one hour at Sandeep's on the computer
Tues	Raining hard, all had a lift to school from Eamon
	At lunchtime, play tag game on school field
	After school, go swimming together – walk there and back and have tea there. Look for birds' nests
Wed	Walk to school quick way.
	Sit together on minibus for school visit to canal museum
	Home from visit late so go straight home together

Thu	Walk to school the long way and look for frogs in the pond	
Fri	Sammy ill so just two of us went to school	
	Lunchtime played rounders on the field	
	After school went to visit Sammy who was better, couldn't stay long so went to play in the park for an hour	
Sat	Swimming and drink at the pool café together from 2 to 4:30. Then played in the park. Allowed to have tea at Sandeep's at 6 o'clock	
Sun	Didn't see each other	

ACTIVITY 45	QUALITY TIME WITH FRIENDS

Allow about 15 minutes

Look at the list of activities the children took part in together. Underline or highlight those that allowed children to be with each other without adult supervision in the way it seems that Bilkis was able to be with her friends.

COMMENT

The children managed to have some time to themselves most days.

It is pleasing to note how much time together these children seem to have compared to what Kiran, one of our daughters, has with her friends. The walks to and from school are important times as they allow the children to do something together, prepare for the day or unwind from it, and get some exercise as well. Having a swimming pool nearby is also good and the children obviously make this into a social occasion as well by having a drink in the café afterwards. Notice how they were also able to get in two sessions of playing in the park.

By contrast, Kiran does not live near any of her school friends, being a good 15-minute walk from the nearest of them. This is a barrier to 'just hanging about' and means she had to rely on adults to take her to and from friends' homes. With longer days and being older, she is now able to walk and meet up with friends at the local leisure centre to go swimming, but she lives a bit too far from them to spontaneously drop in on them, or they on her. A number of her friends live close to each other, and are able to do the kind of things Daisy and her friends do regularly. The worry is that too much adult-initiated or adult-controlled activity could result in children being less able to take responsibility for structuring their lives, which is not helpful to them in the long run.

Another area of children's friendships that adults can try to control is who children choose as their friends. Some parents worry that their child will mix with children from families who don't share the same values as them. But circumstances often dictate how easy it is for children to make and keep friends, and parents need to take account of these so they don't use up energy engineering friendships that might not work out.

4.5 PATTERNS OF FRIENDSHIP

In Brannen and colleagues' study, children generally chose friends who were the same age and sex as themselves. Some explained their gender preference as to do with being able to talk 'girl' or 'boy' talk with them. Bilkis in the video extract also didn't want to mix with boys who she thought of as 'bad'. Jenni Murray, the UK broadcaster, has recently written critically about the 'demonizing' of boys, and how this needs to stop, giving examples of her own sons and others she knows who do not fit the negative stereotypes portrayed of boys as 'exhausting', 'failing', 'vandals', 'lazy', 'irresponsible' (*Guardian*, 5 July 2003).

DAISY'S AND SANDEEP'S VIEWS

Daisy and Sandeep commented on this finding. Daisy said:

> I'm not surprised girls want to stick together. Most of the boys in our class are so weird. They have to have attention all the time and don't respect girls enough. Sandeep is different – he's not pushy and rude and he likes the things we like, so I do agree that some boys can be OK.

Sandeep said:

> I like the boys in my class. We work together in school time but I don't like football and fighting and that's what lots of them like to do. I have always liked to do things that girls also enjoy – dancing, acting, looking at nature. I think if I wasn't good at my work especially at computers then I would get teased more but everyone accepts me as I am.

It can be possible, then, for children to have patterns of friendship that do not conform to what is expected, and challenge our assumptions.

HOW THE SCHOOL CHOICES WORKED OUT

Sandeep did get a place at the school his cousins attended, and was happy to go there. Daisy and Sammy both took the entrance exam for the convent. Sammy passed and was offered a place, but Daisy didn't. Both girls got a place at the local high school. Sammy was so worried at the thought of the travelling and losing her friends and also not pleasing her family that she became ill. Her family said she could go to the local school if she would agree to take private lessons if they felt this necessary. Sammy agreed to this. Daisy and Sammy were very disappointed that Sandeep could not be with them at their new school. They felt he had chosen his cousins rather then them and wouldn't speak to him. Sandeep was very upset at this and told his dad what had happened but didn't want his dad to talk to Daisy and Sammy or their parents. His dad suggested they talk to the children's class teacher to see if this time of the year when school choices are made put a strain on friendships.

Their class teacher was sympathetic and said she could feel the disappointment in the class when children were not going to the same school as their friends, and that there were others in the class similarly affected. She agreed to use 'circle time' to discuss change, friendships and disappointments with the class. This worked well and the children were encouraged to talk about how they felt without anyone being singled out. Daisy and Sammy were able to apologize to Sandeep for hurting his feelings and vowed to keep in touch with him as much as they could when he was at his new school.

Key points

- Children's contribution to families varies, but is often greater than adults think.

- In poorer countries children's contribution can be essential to the family economy.

- The quality of friendships is more important than the number of friends.

Effective study   Essay writing

You have now had two opportunities to practise essay writing and getting feedback on your essays. Hopefully the feedback from your tutor will have helped you to focus on the areas of writing where you need more practice or guidance. Don't be disheartened by constructive criticism; it gives you a focus for improving your writing.

One of the core features of a clear and slick essay is structure. By 'structure' we mean the way in which you divide up your essay into manageable groups of ideas and also lead the reader through your discussion. A good structure can make the difference between a hotchpotch of relevant but unconnected ideas and facts, and a well argued and logical discussion.

In order to check out how well you are structuring your essays, take out your last essay. You may want to photocopy it if you do not want to mark or damage the original. Read through it again and then answer the following:

1   Did you have an introductory paragraph and if so what did it *do or say?*

2   Did you have a concluding paragraph and if so what did it *do or say?*

3   How many paragraphs did you have apart from any introduction or conclusion?

4   Count how many points or ideas were in each paragraph.

5   Finally cut up the paragraphs and if possible ask someone else to try to put it back together. If you do not have anyone to ask, check how easy you think it might be to link each paragraph to the one before and after it.

There are no absolute rules about structuring your essay, and you will probably come across conflicting advice as you move through your higher education. However, here are some guiding principles:

1   An introduction and conclusion *can* be very helpful in organizing your ideas. An introduction should set the scene for the reader, letting them know from the outset how you intend to tackle the question. You can, for example, tell the reader, in brief, the main ideas or examples which you are going to use. If you do this, put them in the order you have covered them so that the reader can look out for them.

2   A conclusion is not a repetition of your introduction. It is the place where you draw your *conclusions* – or, in other words, taking into account all of the ideas and evidence you have discussed in your essay, what is your final point or position in relation to an argument. You may want to briefly revisit highlights of ideas or evidence to justify your position, but the bulk of the discussion should have taken place in your essay. It is not helpful to introduce new ideas or evidence in your conclusion.

3   For the length of essay that you are writing here, three or four paragraphs in addition to your introduction and conclusion is as much as you can expect to write.

4   Each paragraph should develop one main point or idea which contributes towards your argument.

5   This last task is very tricky even with an excellent essay. However, it is worth doing in order to think about what your own logic or reasoning was for ordering the paragraphs in the way that you did. Did you give the reader any help in following your reasoning? It can be helpful to end a paragraph with a short statement which leads the reader on to the beginning of the next paragraph.

When you begin planning your final essay, and then again when you check it before handing it in, check through these five questions again and check out for yourself how well you feel that you have organized your answer.

ACTIVITY 46   **EFFECTIVE STUDY REFLECTIVE ACTIVITY**

Congratulations! You have finished working your way through the study materials for *Understanding Children*. This does not mean that you have finished your studies though – as you still need to complete your assignment. The effectiveness of your studying will be assessed in your essay, but you will also be assessed on how your ability to think about how you study and learn.

As with all your previous assignments, you will need to complete this review on a separate piece of paper, but this time it will be sent off with your end-of-course assessment to the university rather than to your own tutor.

1   Pick one area of *effective study* which you feel more confident about and write down three things that you understand better or are better at doing. For each one write a couple of sentences about how you feel you have improved.

2   Pick one area of studying which you would like to develop further in the future. Try to think of a couple of questions which would help you and write them down along with how you intend to find out the answers.

3   Give an example of two ways in which you have improved the way in which you study as a result of either feedback from your tutor and/or advice from the course materials. You should say what the advice was and how it has assisted you.

CONCLUSION

We hope that you have enjoyed *Understanding Children* and that it has encouraged you to continue with studying, whether in a subject related to children or in a new direction. Whichever area of study you choose, the time that you have spent developing your ability to study effectively should give you a good start.

Mia, Ryan and Daisy, along with the rest of the Family have become very real to all of us in the course team; we need to remind ourselves that they are fictional! Through their eyes and experiences, however, we hope that you have seen children's lives in a slightly different way. You have come across some different opinions about children, but we feel that what comes though is their eternal ability to amaze adults. From babies right through to pre-adolescents, children's ability to communicate and ensure that they are taken account of, despite adults being reluctant or unsure about hearing them at times, is remarkable. While adults remain preoccupied with 'teaching' the children in their care, we hope they will also remember to learn from them.

REFERENCES

BBC TV (2001) *Child of Our Time*, Programme 1 'Thanks for the Memories'

Berry Brazelton, T. and Cramer, B. G. (1991) *The Earliest Relationship*, London: Karnac Books

Birmingham Health Education Unit (2000) *Birmingham Healthy School Standard Guidance for Schools*, Birmingham: Birmingham Education Department

Bliss, T. (1994) *Managing Children, Managing Themselves: Strategies for the classroom and playground*, Avon: Lame Duck

Brannen, J., Heptinstall, E. and Bhopal, K. (2000) *Connecting Children: Care and Family Life in Later Childhood,* London: Routledge Falmer. (Note: Julia Brannen also made a video of discussions with children about the results of her study. This gave the children further chances to express their views on family life. The account of what she did is written up as: Brannen, J. (2002) 'The use of video in research dissemination: children as experts on their own family lives', *International Journal of Social Research Methodology*, vol. 5, no. 2, pp. 173–180)

Children and Young People's Unit (2002) *Your say*, http://www.cypu.gov.uk/consultationresults

Cole, M. (1998) 'Culture in development', in Woodhead, M., Faulkner, D. and Littleton, K. (eds) *Cultural Worlds of Early Childhood*, London: Routledge in association with the Open University

Daniel, B., Wassell, S. and Gilligan, R. (1999) *Child Development for Child Care Protection Workers*, London: Jessica Kingsley

Daniels, L. and McCarraher, L. (no date), *Ask the children: what do children really think of working parents?* (online), http://www.radlogic.demon.co.uk/page23.html to page25.html; accessed 19 October 2003

Department for Education and Employment (DfEE) (1999) *Healthy Schools Standard*, London: HMSO

Department of Health (2002) *Listening, Hearing and Responding*: *Department of Health Action Plan – Core principles for the involvement of children and young people,* www.doh.gov.uk

Dunn, J. and Deater-Deckard, K. (2001) *Children's Views of Their Changing Families*, York: York Publishing Services/Joseph Rowntree Foundation

Fairbairn, G. J. and Fairbairn, S. A. (2001) *Reading at University: A Guide for Students*, Buckingham: Open University Press

Galinsky, E. (1999) *Ask the Children: What America's Children Really Think About Working Parents,* New York: William Morrow and Company

Goldson, B. (2001) 'The demonization of children: from the symbolic to the institutional' in Foley, P., Roche, J. and Tucker, S. (2001) *Children and Society*, Hampshire: Palgrave

Jones, A., Jeyasingham, D. and Rajasooriya, S. (2002) *Invisible Families*, Bristol: Policy Press/JRF

Kohn, A. (1993, 1999) *Punished by Rewards: The Trouble with Gold Stars, Incentive Plans, A's, Praise and Other Bribes*, New York: Houghton Mifflin

Lancaster, P. (2003) *Listening to Young Children*, Buckingham: Open University Press

Mayall, B. (1996) *Children, Health and the Social Order*, Buckingham: Open University Press

Meggitt, C. and Sunderland, G. (2000) *Child Development: An illustrated guide*, London: Heinemann Child Care, pp. 7, 10, 11

Modood, T., Berthoud, R., Lakey, J., Nazroo, J., Smith, P., Virdee, S. and Beishon, S. (1997) *Ethnic Minorities in Britain: Diversity and Disadvantage – Fourth National Survey of Ethnic Minorities*, London: Policy Studies Institute

Morrow, V. (1998) *Understanding Families: Children's Perspectives*, London: National Children's Bureau/Joseph Rowntree Foundation

Murray, J. (2003) '10 myths about boys', *Guardian*, 5 July 2003

NSPCC (2002) 'Encouraging better behaviour' (online), http://www.nspcc.org.uk/html/Home/Needadvice/encouragingbetterbehaviour.htm; accessed 18 October 2003

Oates, J. (ed.) (1994) *The Foundations of Child Development*, Oxford: Blackwell in association with the Open University

Olwig, K. F. (1993) *Global Culture Island Identity: Continuity and Change in the Afro-Caribbean community of Nevis Switzerland*, pp. 146–7, Horwood

Open University (1999) *Student Toolkit 1: The effective use of English*, Milton Keynes: The Open University

Open University (2002) U212 *Childhood*, course material and video 2, Milton Keynes: The Open University

Parentline Plus (no date) *Parents: get information about ... New baby* and *Managing family changes* (online), http://www.parentlineplus.org.uk/data/parents; accessed 18 October 2003

RollerCoaster.ie (2003) *Sleep: star charts approach* (online), http://www.rollercoaster.ie/sleep/star_charts.asp; accessed 18 October 2003

Shropshire, J. and Middleton, S. (1999) *Small Expectations: Learning to be Poor?* York: Joseph Rowntree Foundation

Song, M. (1999) *Helping Out: Children's Labour in Ethnic Businesses*, Philadelphia: Temple University Press

Thomas, N. (2001) 'Listening to children', in Foley, P., Roche, J. and Tucker, S. (eds) *Children and Society*, Hampshire: Palgrave (also Thomas, N., O'Kane, C. and McNeill, S. (1998) *Voices with Volume* (audiotape), Swansea: University of Wales Swansea, International Centre for Childhood Studies)

Triangle (2003) (online), http://www.Triangle-services.co.uk; accessed 19 October 2003

Waksler, F. C. (1996) *The Little Trials of Childhood and Children's Strategies for Dealing with Them*, London: Falmer Press

Woodhead, M. (2003) 'Listen to what children say', in Maybin, J. and Woodhead, M. (eds) *Childhoods in Context*, London: Wiley with the Open University

Zinnecker, J. (2001) 'Pre-adolescent children', in Du Bois-Reymond, M., Sünker, H. and Krüger, H-H. (eds) *Childhood in Europe: Approaches – Trends – Findings*, New York: Peter Lang

ACKNOWLEDGEMENTS

Grateful acknowledgement is made to the following sources for permission to reproduce material within this product.

Text

pp. 128–130: Copyright © Radlogic, www.radlogic.co.uk

Tables

Table 19: Brennan, J. Heptinstal, E. and Kalwant, B. (2000) 'Children's contribution to family life', *Connecting Children Care and Family Life in Later Childhood*. Copyright © Julia Brannen, Ellen Heptinstall and Kalwant Bhopal

Illustrations

Cover: John Burningham

Figure 14: Clarissa Leahy/Photofusion; Figure 15: Bubbles; Figure 24: From *Little Teddy Bear's Happy Face Sad Face: A First Book About Feelings*, copyright © 1998 Printlink Publishing, Inc. Reprinted with permission of The Millbrook Press, Inc. All rights reserved; Figure 26: Copyright © Down's Syndrome Society; Figure 30: Martin Woodhead/The Open University; Figure 31: Copyright © Photodisk; Figure 32: Courtesy of The Center: Milton Keynes; Figure 41: Martin Woodhead/The Open University.

Every effort has been made to contact copyright holders. If any have been inadvertently overlooked the publishers will be pleased to make the necessary arrangements at the first opportunity.